D1593820

Learning
Centers for
Child-Centered
Classrooms

The Authors

Janice Pattillo is Professor of Early Childhood and Elementary Education at Stephen F. Austin State University, Nacogdoches, Texas.

Elizabeth Vaughan is Associate Professor of Early Childhood/ Elementary Education at Stephen F. Austin State University, Nacogdoches, Texas.

The Advisory Panel

Janet O. Cass, Kindergarten Teacher, Destin Elementary School, Florida

Judith A. Cook, Teacher of Neurologically Impaired/Emotionally Disturbed/Elementary Children, Somerville, New Jersey

Sandra L. Gordon, Professor of Elementary and Early Childhood Education, Moorhead State University, Minnesota

Dolores Hattox, First Grade Teacher, Fletcher Elementary School, Beaumont Independent School District, Texas

Evelyn K. Hill, Third Grade Teacher, Auburn, Massachusetts

Laura Schmink, Kindergarten Teacher, St. Louis Public Schools, Missouri

NEA
EARLY CHILDHOOD
EDUCATION SERIES

Learning Centers for Child-Centered Classrooms

Janice Pattillo
Elizabeth Vaughan

A NATIONAL EDUCATION ASSOCIATION
PUBLICATION

3578

Printing History
    First Printing: February 1992
    Second Printing: March 1994

Note

The opinions expressed in this publication should not be construed as representing the policy or position of the National Education Association. Materials published by the NEA Professional Library are intended to be discussion documents for educators who are concerned with specialized interests of the profession.

Library of Congress Cataloging-in-Publication Data

Pattillo, Janice.
  Learning Centers for child-centered classrooms / Janice Pattillo,
Elizabeth Vaughan.
     p.   cm.—(NEA early childhood education series)
  Includes bibliographical references.
  ISBN 0-8106-0357-8
  1. Classroom learning centers—United States—Planning.
  2. Activity programs in education—Handbooks, manuals, etc.
  3. Teaching—Aids and devices—Handbooks, manuals, etc.
I. Vaughan, Elizabeth.   II. Title.   III. Series: Early childhood
education series (Washington, D.C.)
LB3044.82.P38   1992
372.13'078—dc20

91-19538
CIP

CONTENTS

Dedicated to
the past and present teachers of the
Early Childhood Laboratory
at Stephen F. Austin State University,
who have continuously developed and
refined this learning center approach.

Special thanks go to Melanie Partin, illustrator, and Margie Blount, typist. Their untiring assistance and professional skill helped make this effort possible.

Chapter 1

INTRODUCTION

An old Chinese proverb states:

I hear and I forget,
I see, and I remember,
I do, and I understand.

Learning centers provide a classroom organization that facilitates doing and understanding.

The National Association for the Education of Young Children (NAEYC), in its position statement on developmentally appropriate practices in early childhood, calls for a curriculum of active learning organized around learning centers for four- to eight-year-olds. For four- and five-year-olds, teaching strategies include the following:

- Children select many of their own activities from among a variety of learning areas the teacher prepares, including dramatic play, blocks, science, math, games and puzzles, books, recordings, art, and music.

- Children are expected to be physically and mentally active. Children choose from among activities the teacher has set up or the children spontaneously initiate.

- Children work individually or in small, informal groups most of the time.

- Children are provided concrete learning activities with materials and people relevant to their own life experiences. (1, p. 54)*

---

*Numbers in parentheses appearing in the text refer to the Bibliography beginning on page 175.

For the primary grades, first through third, appropriate teaching strategies include projects and learning centers.

The curriculum is integrated so that children's learning in all traditional subject areas occurs primarily through projects and learning centers that teachers plan and that reflect children's interests and suggestions. Teachers guide children's involvement in projects and enrich the learning experience by extending children's ideas, responding to their questions, engaging them in conversation, and challenging their thinking. (1, p. 68)

WHAT ARE THE ADVANTAGES OF USING LEARNING CENTERS?

The learning center approach to teaching is most appropriate for young children because it promotes the development of autonomy which, according to Piaget (14), should be the goal of education. Autonomy is developed because children are active; they learn at their own pace; they make choices; they are self-directed rather than teacher-directed; they assume responsibility for learning; they practice freedom within limits. In addition, children gain other advantages in a learning center classroom. Learning centers provide opportunities for children to learn through concrete experiences with "real" objects. Because children have choices, they are more intrinsically motivated to learn. Children have more opportunities for social interaction with their peers. This leads to cooperative learning, peer teaching, and the development of many social skills. Learning centers also provide for more oral language development as children verbalize their actions and discuss problems and solutions with others.

Teachers as well find advantages in using learning centers. Learning centers enable the teacher to meet the individual needs of all children. Materials and activities in the classroom reflect a variety of skill levels so that the children may choose those appropriate to their own level and achieve success in the classroom. This allows the teacher to meet the needs of a diverse group of children in the classroom, including main-streamed children, limited English proficiency children, and children of diverse racial and ethnic backgrounds. Learning centers enable the teacher to integrate skills from various academic disciplines into activities that are meaningful and purposeful to the child. Because activities are child-directed, not teacher-directed, the teacher is free to interact with children in a one-on-one or small-group situation. This allows the teacher to observe children's skills and problem areas more closely. And, finally, multiple sets of materials are not needed because only a few children at a time may be using them in a center area.

WHAT ARE LEARNING CENTERS?

A learning center is a defined space where materials are organized in such a way that children learn without the teacher's constant presence and direction. Many terms are used inter-changeably with learning centers, including *interest centers, learning stations, activity areas, free-choice areas, booths,* and *enrichment centers.* Each of these terms indicates varied amounts of structure and organization. The term *learning center* can be confused with specifically designated rooms or buildings, such as learning resource centers, instructional materials centers, curricu-lum centers, media centers, and multipurpose centers. However, in this book, learning center refers to a place (usually a small area) within the classroom where children interact with materials and other children to develop certain learnings. Activities in each learning center are planned by the teacher according to the assessed needs of the children.

WHAT DOES A LEARNING CENTER CLASSROOM LOOK LIKE?

Imagine opening the door to a first grade classroom organized into learning centers. Eleven small areas are defined by shelves and tables. These separate areas are art, blocks, dramatic play, creative writing, handwriting, spelling, reading, math, science, library, and construction. Materials are attractively displayed on the shelves and tables. Self-directing charts with pictures and words tell children what to do in each area. The children work independently or in small groups. The teacher interacts informally in several centers and then takes a small group of children to a corner of the room to focus on a particular activity. As she works with the children, the teacher records information about each child's development on a clipboard. The other children continue to work in various centers, changing to new centers as they finish activities. After about an hour and a half, the teacher calls the group to the group area, reviews planning sheets, and discusses where the children will work during center time in the afternoon.

Learning centers are not new. John Dewey's philosophy of progressive education in the early 1900s emphasized "learning by doing." Dewey and Dewey (2) described an educational curriculum that was active, based on the child's experience and interests, initiated by the child, and integrated into meaningful activities. "The teacher and the book are no longer the only instructors; the hands, the eyes, the ears, in fact the whole body becomes sources of information . . . " (p. 74).

Learning centers are not the easiest way to organize a classroom. The use of learning centers represents a philosophy of education—a commitment to individualized, self-directed, and individually constructed knowledge. If a teacher believes that children learn primarily from others—from knowledge being given to another mainly from telling—then that teacher will not find learning centers worth the effort required to set them up.

But if a teacher believes that children construct knowledge from interactions with materials and other people, and that children should be autonomous, self-directing, responsible individuals, then the classroom will be organized so that these characteristics will be enhanced. Learning centers provide a vehicle for such development.

Chapter 2

ORGANIZATION AND MANAGEMENT

The organization and the management of learning centers are two of the most important tasks of a teacher. During the planning phase, important decisions must be made about arranging the room, scheduling the day, previewing and reviewing activities, limiting center numbers, and monitoring center choices. Each of these components of organization and management combines to make the classroom function effectively. To assist in the decision making, each of these topics is discussed separately in this chapter.

ARRANGING THE ROOM

First of all, when arranging the room, the teacher must decide how many center areas are needed. This number is determined by the age and the developmental needs of the children, as well as by the required grade-level content. Several additional questions must be answered. If all of the children are in centers at one time, how many extra spaces beyond the number of children are needed so that children can change centers? Which centers should be grouped together? How may existing desks, tables, and shelves be used? Are different centers more appropriate for certain age groups? Where will children meet as a total group?

In our school, we increase the number of centers with each succeeding age group. The preprimary (prekindergarten, kindergarten) centers are categorized according to the type of activities involved in each. The primary (first through third grade) centers are usually categorized according to subject matter.

With each succeeding age group, centers become more specific and differentiated (Figure 1). For example, to develop language skills, we begin with a library center in prekindergarten, emphasizing oral language and picture reading. In kindergarten, the library center becomes two separate areas, the library and the communication centers, stressing early literacy skills in communication. In the primary grades, the library and communication centers are divided into the more academic areas related to the language arts: reading, handwriting, creative writing, spelling, and library.

The following factors should be considered when organizing the room:

1. Active and quiet centers should be separated. Preprimary active centers include music, blocks, dramatic play, construction, and gross motor activities. Preprimary quiet centers include art, discovery, library, table games, communication, and mathematics. Primary active centers include art, blocks, dramatic play, and music. Primary quiet centers include creative writing, reading, handwriting, spelling, library, mathematics, science, and social studies.
2. Compatible centers should be placed next to each other. Both art and construction may need to be located near the water source. Blocks and dramatic play can be combined to enhance play. For example, the hollow blocks may be used to build shelves for the grocery store.
3. Incompatible centers should be separated for younger children. Construction and blocks may need to be separated so that children do not use the blocks in woodworking activities. Art materials may need to be kept separate from books in the library center.

Figure 1

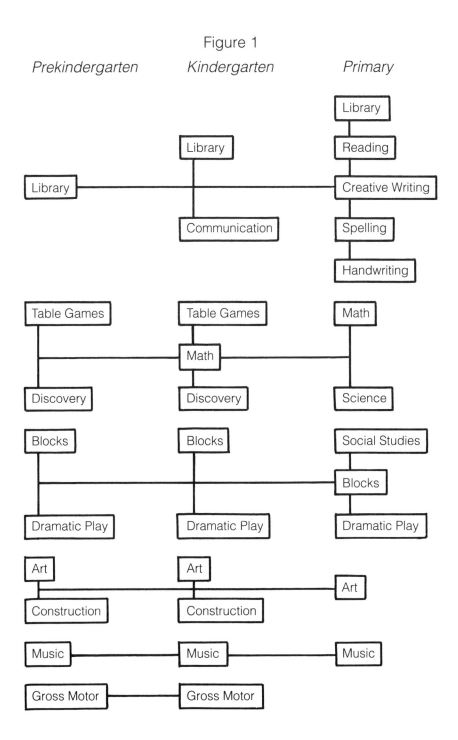

4. Centers should be large enough that additional spaces are available when all children are working. This allows children freedom to change centers as needed.
5. A large-group meeting place should be established.
6. Fixed properties of the room, such as water, windows, doors, and electrical outlets, should be considered.
7. Traffic flow patterns should be considered. High-traffic areas around doors, restrooms, and water fountains should have pathways for easy access. Children should be able to move around the room without having to walk through other centers and disrupt children who are working.
8. Low cabinets and dividers provide separate areas and lessen visual distractions.
9. Each center needs table or floor work space and shelving that holds several activities.
10. Space is needed for personal items such as coats, artwork, and projects.
11. Storage of teacher materials must be considered. Learning centers use many hands-on materials, which can be stored in boxes of consistent size and used as room dividers.
12. The room should balance the use of space in a harmonious way. There should be an open appearance, but large areas of unused space should be avoided.

An example of a kindergarten classroom is shown in Figure 2. Figure 3 shows an example of a primary classroom. For a teacher who is just beginning to move into a centers approach, but wants to retain individual desks, the arrangement shown in Figure 4 can be used. Each square represents a desk. During center time, children move to desks of other children.

Figure 2

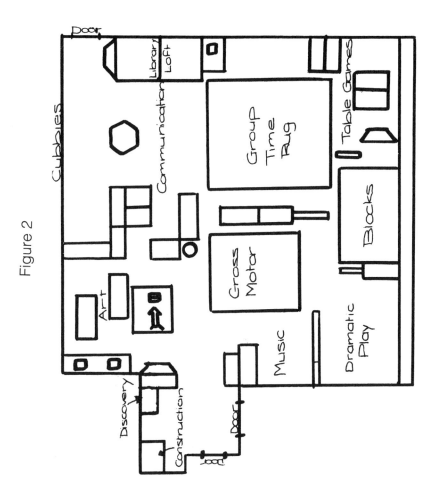

21

Figure 3

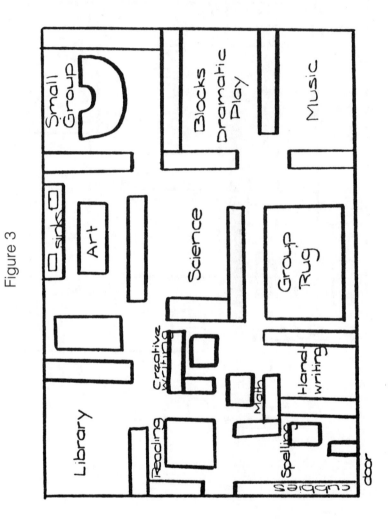

Figure 4

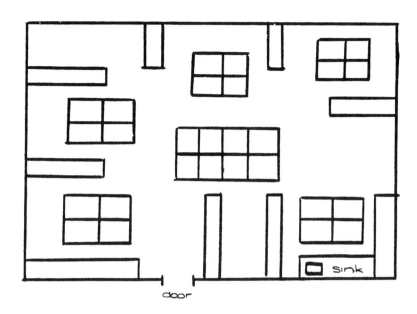

door

SCHEDULING THE DAY

After the room is arranged, a major consideration is planning the daily schedule. A large block of time should be allotted for learning center activities. In the preprimary classroom, usually 1 to 1¹/₂ hours are needed. First through third grade children need longer blocks of time for learning centers. In our school, primary children spend two hours in centers in the morning and one to two hours in the afternoon. This learning center activity period includes time for the preview and review of centers, the transitions to and from centers, and cleanup. During learning center time, children move at their own pace through the center activities they select. Also, the teacher may pull small groups of children for teacher-directed instruction, while other children work individually.

A typical preprimary schedule might look like this:

8:00 – 8:15	Arrival (feed pets, water plants, share books at the group area)
8:15 – 8:35	Language experience activity
8:35 – 10:05	Preview of centers
	Learning center activities
	Small-group instruction
	Cleanup
	Review of centers
10:05 – 10:25	Group music
10:25 – 10:55	Outside play
10:55 – 11:15	Group story
11:15 – 11:45	Lunch
11:45 – 12:45	Rest time
12:45 – 1:05	Group story
1:05 – 2:25	Preview of centers
	Learning center activities
	Small-group instruction
	Cleanup
	Review of centers
2:25 – 2:45	Group music
2:45 – 3:00	Preparation for leaving
3:00 – 5:00	Extended day activities
	Outside play
	Group story
	Limited centers

A typical primary schedule might look like this:

8:00 – 8:15	Arrival (feed pets, water plants, share books at the group area)
8:15 – 8:45	Group planning
	Story dictation
8:45 – 10:45	Preview of centers
	Learning center activities
	Small-group reading (with teacher direction)
	Cleanup
	Review of centers
10:45 – 11:00	Story
11:00 – 11:30	Physical education

11:30 – 12:00	Lunch
12:00 – 1:00	Bathroom and rest
1:00 – 1:30	Music/social studies/science/health
1:30 – 2:50	Preview of centers
	Learning center activities
	Small-group math
	Cleanup
	Review of centers
2:50 – 3:00	Preparation for leaving
3:00 – 5:00	Extended day activities
	Outside play
	Group story
	Limited centers

PREVIEWING AND REVIEWING ACTIVITIES

Preview and review are major components of the learning center time. During these two important times, the teacher should plan with the children as a total group. During preview, the teacher

1. Tells the children about new activities in each center.
2. Discusses how equipment is used.
3. Establishes rules using open–ended questions, such as "Why is it important for the game markers to be kept in the box?" and leads discussions.
4. Anticipates problems and discusses how they can be avoided.
5. Stimulates interest in particular activities.
6. Models how to play certain games or roles, such as in dramatic play.

During review, the teacher

1. Praises appropriate behavior.
2. Encourages children to tell about or show their work from center time.

25

3. Reviews the plan sheets to check children's self–pacing (primary).
4. Sets goals for future learning center times.

LIMITING CENTER NUMBERS

After preview, children should be allowed a few at a time to select the center in which they will begin working. During the one to two hours set aside for learning centers, children should move freely from center to center as long as space permits.

In order to monitor the number of children in each center, a system of organization should be established. One way to do this is with a center planning board, with pictures and hooks that indicate center spaces (Figure 5). For example, the art center might have four hooks, indicating space for four children. The child hangs his name or picture on the board when he goes to the center. If all the hooks for a particular center are filled, the child must choose another center. After hanging his name, the child goes to that area of the room and begins to work. When the child is ready to change centers, he returns to the planning board and changes the placement of his name.

Another way to limit center numbers is to hang a board with a picture and the name of the center beside each center area. Children hang their names at each individual center rather than at a central planning board (Figure 6).

Another option is to color-code each center and place corresponding colored clothespins on the board posted at each center (Figure 7). The number of clothespins represents the number of children that can be in that center at one time. Children place the clothespins on their clothes. With this system, the teacher can tell at a glance who should be in the center and who should not by looking at the colored clothespins. Bracelets made from colored buttons and elastic can be used in a similar manner (Figure 8). The correct number of bracelets would be placed in a small basket or container at each center.

26

Figure 5

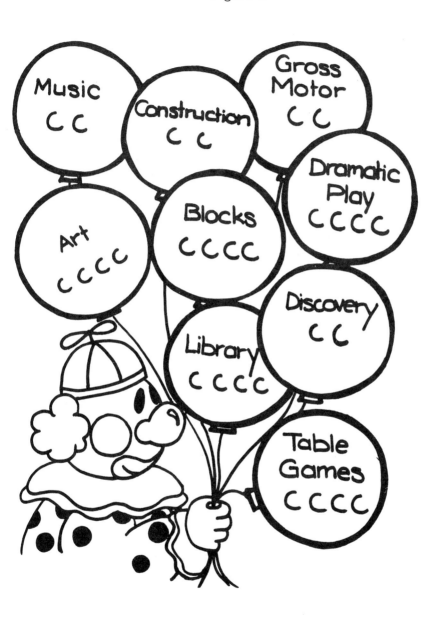

Figure 6

Figure 7

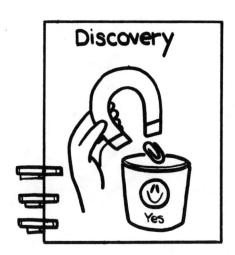

Figure 8

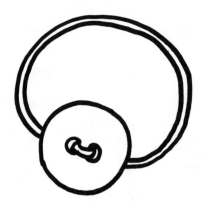

MONITORING CENTER CHOICES

Teachers might want to monitor the choices children make in order to assure exposure to a variety of activities and skills. In a kindergarten classroom, each child could use a weekly plan form, such as that shown in Figure 9. These forms can be kept in mailboxes labeled for each child beside the planning board. As the child chooses a center, she colors in a space beside that particular center. When all spaces are colored beside a center, that center is no longer an option for the child that week. In this way, the teacher can limit the number of times per week a child can visit a particular area, yet the child still is able to make choices about the centers in which she will work. Each week a new plan form is provided.

In a primary classroom, children might be required to visit each of the quiet centers each day. A daily plan form, such as that shown in Figure 10, might be used. In this case, the child would color in a center as he completes the number of activities specified on the plan sheet for that area. With this system, the teacher can check a child's plan sheet at any time during center time and see how much work the child has completed. Active centers are available to the child only after work in quiet centers has been completed.

There are always a few children who waste time during center time and do not complete all of their work. Learning to responsibly complete assigned centers and individually assigned activities is a very important learning for primary children. To facilitate the development of responsibility, the teacher might need to collect all five of the plan sheets for each child at the end of the week. She should also collect the shelf checklists placed beside each activity that is assigned to specific children (see Chapter 5). If a teacher changes an activity at the end of the week and notices that certain children have not checked the shelf checklist, she should collect the checklist with the activity. The teacher should bring the plan sheets and shelf checklists to the

Figure 9

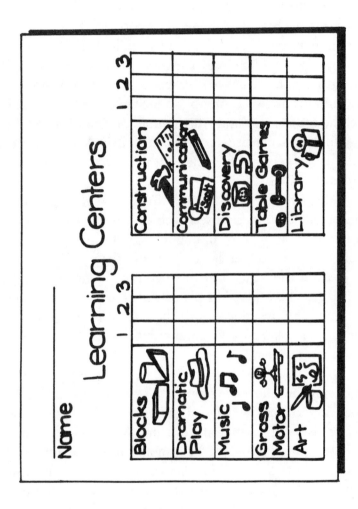

Cheryl Patterson, Early Childhood Laboratory, Stephen F. Austin State University.

30

Figure 10

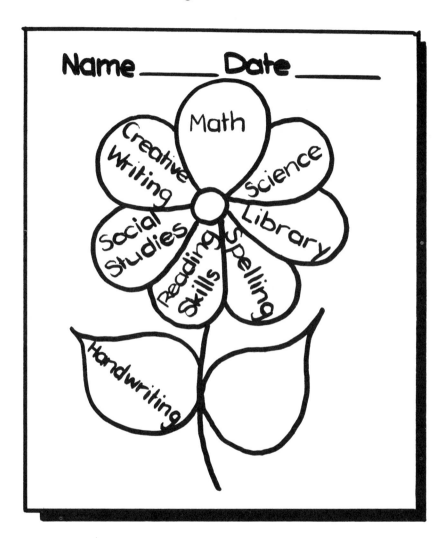

group meeting at preview or review time and make plans for completing work.

The teacher can then provide a time for children to complete unfinished activities. Often the work can be finished on Friday, while children who have completed their work do self-selected activities. After a few weeks, children realize that finishing work in centers allows them to have other choices.

During learning center time, it is very important for the teacher to take time to check for children who rush through activities, encouraging them to take their time. After several weeks, teachers have a feel for those children who need to move faster, those who need to slow down, and those who need to work at staying on task.

The learning center classroom must be well organized in order to function effectively. These are some of the techniques that might be used to assist the teacher. Other similar techniques might also be used. Each teacher must plan and develop a system of organization that will work with his group of children and in his particular classroom situation.

Chapter 3

TEACHER ROLES

The teacher's role in a learning center classroom is very different from that in a traditional classroom. She now must arrange an environment that facilitates children's self-directed learning, rather than being the focal point of the learning activity. In a traditional classroom, the teacher directs the lesson and presents information to the total group. In a learning center classroom, only a small amount of time is spent in total-group situations. In a learning center classroom, children work independently or in small groups with the various materials and activities available. The teacher moves around the classroom to the various centers and becomes involved in activities for short periods of time. The teacher roles discussed in this chapter include

- *Assessment:* The teacher evaluates children's learning.
- *Planning:* The teacher plans appropriate learning activities.
- *Set-Up:* The teacher prepares and arranges materials/activities in the centers.
- *Interaction:* The teacher interacts with children while working in centers.
- *Arbitration:* The teacher works with children to settle disputes. (5)

ASSESSMENT

Assessment refers to the process of evaluation. Learning center classrooms pose a particular problem in the area of assessment. Children work in many different areas of the classroom and on many different activities. How can the teacher monitor what is being learned by each child?

Much of the teacher's assessment is done through informal observation. As the teacher moves from center to center, he watches to see what children are capable of doing and what areas of difficulty are apparent. He might also ask questions of the child to try to determine the child's skill level.

It is important for the teacher to record this information as it is observed. Various systems of recordkeeping can be used. Individual folders might be kept at each center, in which the teacher records information or places samples of children's work. Figure 11 shows an example of an individual assessment sheet. Another method is to have a clipboard with an assessment sheet, such as that shown in Figure 12. All the children's names can be listed on one sheet, and specific skills can be assessed. The assessment sheet is changed weekly as different skills are emphasized in that classroom.

In the primary grades, children might need to turn in written papers or worksheets for teacher evaluation. Again, individual folders can be used, in which children can place their work. Another way to collect papers is to have a basket or box at each center, in which children place their work when completed. In this approach, papers can easily be collected at the end of the period for teacher grading. Another method that can be utilized is to allow children to self-correct or check their partner's work, using an answer sheet. These papers can then be placed in the basket for the teacher to review (3, 5).

The assessment phase provides important information for the next role of the teacher, which is planning. The teacher cannot plan appropriate learning center activities without first knowing the children's level of knowledge and skill development. Which skills are presenting difficulty for children and need continued emphasis in activities? Which skills have been mastered? Which new skills are children ready to begin?

Figure 11
Readiness
Math Assessment

Name _____ Classroom _____ Date _____

Dates			Math Process	Example	Notes
Start	Check				
			Shapes (Identifies)		

			Counting
			   Rote Counting
			   Objects
				1 to 10	

			Numeral Recognition	1 to 10	
			Patterning	Copy model Extend model	

			Sets
			   Matches
			   Recognizes
			   Identifies
			   Reproduces
				Constructs to 10
				with counters	

			Size	Smaller/Larger Same/Different Longest/Shortest Tallest/Shortest	
			Money (Identifies)	Penny Nickel Dime Quarter Dollar	
			Ordinals (Recognizes)	First Second Third Last Middle	
			Fractions	Half of object	
			Number Conservation	O O O O O O O OOOOOOO	

_____
Teacher's Signature

Figure 12
Assessment Tally Sheet

Elements

Children's Names

1. _____									
2. _____									
3. _____									
4. _____									
5. _____									
6. _____									
7. _____									
8. _____									
9. _____									
10. _____									
11. _____									
12. _____									
13. _____									
14. _____									
15. _____									
16. _____									
17. _____									
18. _____									
19. _____									
20. _____									
21. _____									
22. _____									
23. _____									
24. _____									

✔ = can   X = cannot   / = needs help

PLANNING

In the planning phase, the teacher begins by selecting needed objectives, which have been identified during the assessment process. From this list of objectives, activities for each center are planned that highlight or emphasize those particular learnings. Every activity selected should have a specific learning purpose that relates to the objectives listed (5). Figure 13 shows a sample plan sheet for the kindergarten classroom. The list of objectives comes from the essential elements designated for Texas public schools. Each learning center activity relates back to one or more essential elements. For example, in Figure 13, essential elements related to shape are highlighted in the art center through sponge printing with sponges cut in various shapes, shape puzzles in the table games center, shape-patterning activities in the math center, flannelboard shapes in the library center, and tracing shape templates in the communication center.

An example of a primary plan sheet is shown in Figure 14 (pp. 40–41).

SET-UP

After planning the learning center activities, the teacher must arrange the materials for each activity in the learning centers. Since children will be working independently, each center must be set up in such a way that it is self-directing. Children must be able to walk into a center and determine what they are supposed to do and begin work without teacher assistance.

Symbol charts aid in self-direction. These charts combine the use of picture symbols and words to give the child direction (5). At the preprimary level, the picture symbol usually precedes the words (Figure 15). At the primary level, the words usually precede the picture symbols (Figure 16). These symbol charts

Figure 13

SFA EARLY CHILDHOOD LABORATORY — Kindergarten Plan Sheet		
Learning Center Activities	Monday	Tuesday
Art	Easel Painting	Sponge Printing
Blocks	Building Roads unit blocks, rubber cars and trucks, traffic signs,	
Construction	Junk Collage—different sized and shaped objects	
Dramatic Play	Grocery Store check-out counter, sacks, cash register, ads, purses,	
Music	Scarf Dancing—scarves, dance tapes, tape recorder	
Library	"Three Billy Goats Gruff" book and story masks, Flannelboard and flannel shape pieces	
Communication	Journal Writing, Tracing Shape Templates, "Me" Books—	
Table Games	Parquetry, shape puzzles, sequence pictures, Legos,	
Math	Size ordering game, piggy bank counting, shape	
Discovery	Pouring and measuring water table and water using various sized containers	
Gross Motor	Suspended yarn balls with hose paddles	

Essential Elements to Be Highlighted:

English/Language Arts	Math	Science/Health
Listen to instructions and important information Engage in creative drama Discriminate shapes Respond to stories—sequencing/retelling Recognize that writing can entertain and inform	Counting objects Identifying patterns Size and shape relationships Classification Ordering	Observe size and shape of objects Classify objects Arrange events in sequential order Nutritional health Self-concept

Figure 13 *(continued)*

DATES _____ TO_____

Wednesday	Thursday	Friday
Gadget Printing	Shape Collage—paper	Shape Collage—fabric
highway and road pictures		
(milk jug lids, straws cut in different sizes, yarn pieces, wood blocks, etc.)		
wallets, food cans/boxes, shopping basket, play money, coupons, etc.		
Add story puzzles	Add "Shape Story" tape	
paper, writing utensils, magazines, glue, scissors		
Tinkertoys, shape lotto, "Three Bears" size sorting		
patterning, stringing beads with pattern cards		
Shape Sorting (attribute blocks)	Sorting healthy/unhealthy foods	Making peanut butter/ raisin crackers
Social Studies	Fine Arts	Physical Education
Recognize safety symbols Identify basic economic wants—food Express relative size Recognize symbols and models represent real things	Discover shape by seeing and feeling objects Express self in painting and printmaking Use rhythmic and imitative movement Sing songs	Nonlocomotor movements Manipulative skills Eye-hand coordination Spatial awareness

Figure 14

SFA EARLY CHILDHOOD LABORATORY — Primary Plan Sheet

Learning Center Activities	Monday	Tuesday
Creative Writing	Journal writing, Mystery Box, Smell Sack, How Do You	
Handwriting	Etch-a-Sketch, Draw your family and write names,	
Library	Books, newspaper, Story puppets, Record-a-Story,	
Reading Skills	Monopoly Jr., Alphabet Roll Trail Game, Concentration	
Spelling	Boggle Jr., Stamp Out Words, Alphabet Macaroni,	
Math	Touchdown, 40 Chips, Tic-Tac-Toe, Fill the Cup,	
Science	Which Weighs More?, Jelly Beans Graph, Waterdrops,	
Social Studies	Map the Room, Building the School, "Me" Books,	
Blocks	Create an Office—hollow blocks, telephones, paper,	
Dramatic Play	Shoe Store—shoes, boxes, counter, cash register,	
Music	Musical Stage Show—stage platform, microphones,	
Art	Marbled chalk, Collage, Easel painting	
Construction	Paper Bag Puppets—paper sacks, markers, yarn, fabric,	

Essential Elements to Be Highlighted:

English/Language Arts	Math	Science/Health
Identify rhythm and rhyme	Order numbers	Observe similarities and
Engage in creative drama	Add whole numbers	differences
Use word attack skills	Use skip counting	Measure objects
Select books		Classify objects
Use writing conventions		Self-concept
Write descriptions		Cleanliness practices
		Recognize hazards

40

Figure 14 *(continued)*

DATES _____ TO _____

Wednesday	Thursday	Friday
Feel?, Family Names, "If I Were a . . . . "		
Ping Pong Tong, Autograph Book, Telephone Books		
Phone Book/Telephones, A-Z Puzzle		
with Letters, Word Rhymes, Go Fish with letter cards		
Letter Blocks, Stikki Wikki Words		
1-to-10 Order Cards		
Spice Cards, Make Feely Books		
Paper Plate Faces, Name Concentration		
writing utensils, typewriter, envelopes		
foot measurer, play money, receipt book		
tape of popular music, tape recorder, costumes		
construction paper, glue, scissors		

Social Studies	Fine Arts	Physical Education
Identify positive traits of of self and others Know geography of school campus Use graphs	Express individual thoughts and feelings with media Explore vocal sounds Sing songs Dramatize stories using puppetry	Nonlocomotor movements Manipulative skills Eye-hand coordination Creative rhythms

Figure 16

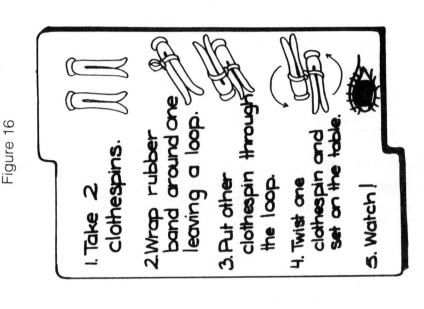

1. Take 2 clothespins.

2. Wrap rubber band around one leaving a loop.

3. Put other clothespin through the loop.

4. Twist one clothespin and set on the table.

5. Watch!

Figure 15

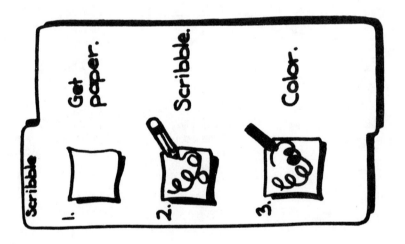

Scribble

1. Get paper.

2. Scribble.

3. Color.

42

illustrate examples of sequential direction activities. They direct the child in the steps of the activity—first, second, third. Some charts may show a single direction or picture of an activity, such as that shown in Figure 17.

There is also a group of charts that use universal symbols (Figure 18). These charts are not tied to specific activities, but can be used in various activities or circumstances (5). These include a chart for each of the five senses and a chart for each sense with a slash mark over it. The "hand" chart and the "no eye" chart may be used with a feel-box activity suggesting, "Use your hands, not your eyes." The "?" symbol tells the child to find out or solve the problem. The "likeness" chart directs the child to find the ones that are the same. The "closed" chart could be posted on particular activities, materials, equipment, or centers that are closed to the children that day (5). These symbol charts can be introduced with activities during the preview of centers.

Other techniques can be used to encourage self-direction. Pictures that will stimulate ideas might be mounted and posted in a center. For example, in the blocks center, pictures of various types of buildings—skyscrapers, homes, log cabins, etc.—may stimulate different types of building by the children.

Self-correction is also a part of self-direction as children move into the primary grades. The teacher is not always present in a center to provide feedback to the child. Many activities and games may be made self-correcting so that children can check their own work. Answer sheets may also be available for a child or partner to check work (3).

Materials placed in a center can be outlined on laminated poster board with transparency markers and labeled. With nonreaders, picture symbols may be drawn inside the outlines. In this way, cleanup also becomes self-directing. Children can see where to return materials and equipment so that center areas remain neat and orderly. The time spent outlining and organizing is regained during cleanup because children can easily find where things belong.

Figure 18

Figure 17

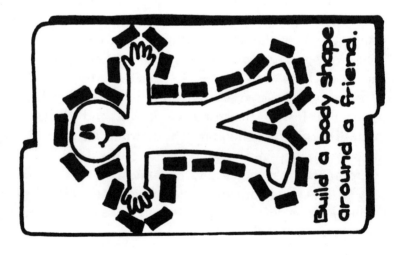

Build a body shape around a friend.

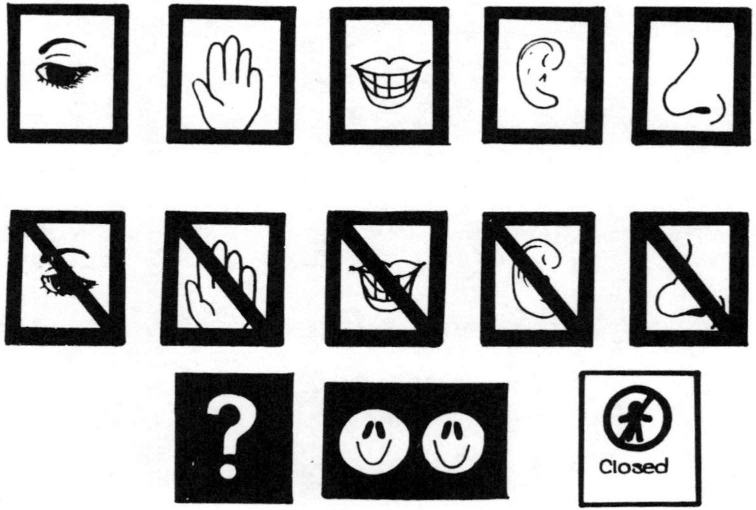

Once activities are set up in the learning centers, children will be able to go to the various centers and begin work on their own without direct teacher involvement. However, during the learning center time, the teacher will be moving among the children to observe and stimulate learning.

INTERACTION

The teacher interacts with the children in a variety of ways during the learning center period through observation, nondirective statements, questioning, directive statements, and physical intervention. These ways reflect various levels of teacher involvement (18).

Observing children during learning center activities is the method of teacher interaction with the least involvement. In this approach, the teacher does not intrude in the child's work. She may be assessing the children's abilities through observation. She also provides supportive looking. Children may work more constructively when they realize the teacher is watching and supporting what they are doing (18).

At the next level of teacher involvement, the teacher interacts through the use of nondirective statements. Now the teacher comments on the children's work, but does not require any response on the part of the child. He might be describing what children are doing or what is happening in the center. He can also use positive reinforcement (10, 18). Examples of nondirective statements are

> "You're using the red paint."
> "The blocks fell down."
> "You've almost finished the math problems."
> "That's a long story you've written."
> "You're really working hard."

Another type of teacher interaction is questioning. Now the teacher is requiring a response from the child. Two types of questions are used. Closed questions require a "right" answer or "yes/no" response. Some examples of closed questions are

"What color is this?"

"What is 3 + 3?"

"Did you finish the story?"

Too often teachers focus on closed questions in order to assess children's knowledge. In learning center classrooms, teachers put more emphasis on open-ended questions, which have more than one possible answer. These questions encourage more language development and thinking on the part of the child (5, 9, 18). Some examples of open-ended questions are

"Tell me about your picture."

"How are these alike/different?"

"What do you think happened first?"

"Why is he sad?"

"How does this work?"

"Why do you think . . . ?"

"What will happen if . . . ?"

Questions are used to determine the level of the child's thinking. Wrong answers should be accepted, not corrected by the teacher. The child will self-correct through continued experience and feedback from peers and the child. "The confrontation of points of view serves to enhance children's ability to reason at increasingly higher levels" (6, p. 36).

The next type of teacher interaction is directive statements. In using directive statements, the teacher is becoming more involved in the child's work. While directions are often given in the form of a symbol chart, these types of statements are used by the teacher when children are having difficulty directing their own behavior. The teacher may give directions such as

"Pretend you are the patient."

"Write a story about this picture."

"Weigh these objects to find the heaviest."

The teacher can also set limits and state rules to the child. For example,

"Keep the paint on the paper."

"Clean up the math games" (18).

The last type of teacher interaction requires the greatest involvement on the part of the teacher. In physical intervention, the teacher becomes physically involved in the center activities. She might model for the children how to work in the center by playing a game with a child or reading a book to a child. She might also have to physically assist a child—for example, helping a child cut with scissors or physically removing a child from a problem situation (18).

Most teachers use a combination of these interaction techniques. In the beginning of the school year, more teacher involvement may be needed than later in the year after children have become used to working on their own. Some children might need more teacher direction than others do. Also, some activities might need more involvement from the teacher than others do (18).

ARBITRATION

As the teacher interacts with children during the learning center period, he may have to settle disputes through arbitration. As children move around the room and work in small groups, conflicts will naturally arise. The teacher's role as an arbitrator is to assist children in resolving these conflicts. He encourages the children to verbalize their feelings and seek appropriate solutions to the problem. The teacher does not solve the problems for the children, but guides the children toward a cooperative resolution.

47

As children learn alternative behaviors for handling conflicts, less assistance from the teacher will be required (5). If autonomy is the goal of education, and if children are to be governed by themselves, rather than by others, they must be allowed to self-correct (6). This response occurs over time, rather than immediately. For instance, in our primary classroom, children play many games in pairs. Occasionally one child might cheat. When the other child becomes aware of this, an argument ensues. The teacher encourages the children to tell each other how they feel and asks the children if they want to continue to play. What we have found is that cheating children will eventually realize that they have few people to play with if they continue to cheat, and thus they change their behavior.

The teacher in a learning center classroom must fulfill many roles. She first assesses the needs of her children. Then she plans appropriate activities to develop various skills. Materials and equipment used in these activities must be set up in a way that will facilitate self-direction. During the learning center activity period, the teacher interacts with the children in a variety of ways, including observing, questioning, and commenting on children's work. She must help to arbitrate conflicts that arise between children. As the children work, she makes assessments that will then affect the next week's plan. Although the teacher is not the focal point in the classroom, her ability to perform these roles effectively is critical to the functioning of the learning center classroom.

Chapter 4

PREPRIMARY LEARNING CENTERS

The basic preprimary learning centers were listed in Chapter 2. Each of these learning centers stimulates the child's development in all areas: physical, intellectual, language, social, emotional, and aesthetic. One of the advantages to using learning centers is that the teacher can integrate skills from these various developmental areas into many activities. As we look at each center individually, we will discuss: (1) the rationale—why the center is important and how developmental skills are integrated into that area, (2) organization—suggestions for how to arrange the center, and (3) sample activities that might be used in the center.

LIBRARY CENTER

Rationale

The primary purpose of the library center is to develop language and literacy skills in a meaningful context. Children develop the oral language skills of speaking and listening through conversing with others, retelling or dramatizing stories, using puppets, listening to stories on tape, matching rhyming words, matching sounds to pictures, and following directions. Emerging literacy skills in reading and writing are developed through experiences with print using books, flannelboard letters, magnetic letters, paper and writing utensils, typewriters, and symbol charts.

In addition to the many language and literacy skills developed in the library center, other skill areas are also integrated. Children develop the cognitive skills of recalling and sequencing as they participate in storytelling activities. Auditory and visual discrimination skills are developed through activities with sounds, shapes, and letters. Classification skills can be developed through activities in which children match appropriate props with characters in a story.

Physical development skills include skills of fine motor development as children manipulate puppets, flannelboard pieces, and magnetic letters. They are also using chalk and other writing utensils.

Socially and emotionally, children learn skills of cooperation through the coordination of puppetry or dramatization roles. They share and take turns with materials. They might develop feelings of empathy with characters in the stories, and they attach positive emotional feelings to their experience with books.

Aesthetically, children develop skills in creative drama through puppetry and dramatization activities. They use imitative sounds and expressive voice tone in their role-playing activities.

Organization

The library center should be in a quiet, well-lighted area of the classroom. Soft furnishings such as carpet, large pillows, and beanbag chairs should be used to give the center a comfortable, cozy feeling. This will invite children to participate in the many language and literacy activities available. Included in the activities in the center each week is a supply of books (15–20) for children to look at or "read" alone, with a friend, or with a teacher. Picture books that are durable and have large, attractive pictures are most appropriate. Books in the library center should be multiethnic, multiracial, and nonsexist. Additional activities should be available for children in the library center. The teacher may wish to always have one storytelling activity available, using flannelboards, puppets, sequence pictures, or other props. She may also want to provide at least one literacy activity, using writing utensils such as a chalkboard and chalk, paper and pencils, typewriters, or magnetic letters. If space permits, it is also good to include a separate listening area where children can use headphones to listen to stories or other tapes.

In our kindergarten classroom, the teacher has divided the library center into two centers—library and communication. In the library center, the teacher emphasizes the oral language skills of speaking and listening, and in the communication center the teacher emphasizes the written language skills of reading and writing. It is important to remember that prior to kindergarten, children should be engaged primarily in oral language activities. During the kindergarten year, increasing emphasis is placed on emerging literacy skills and readiness activities, but oral language development should continue to be a major part of the child's involvement. A sketch of a typical library center set-up is shown in Figure 19.

Activities

Oral Language Activities

- Sound tape: Use tapes of sounds such as animals, instruments, or environmental sounds, and have children identify the source of the noise by selecting matching picture cards.
- Story tape: Use tapes of children's stories, and have corresponding books for children to follow as they listen.
- Instructions tape: Have taped instructions, such as "Clap your hands two times; put two fingers on your head," for children to follow.
- Rhyming concentration: Have picture cards that represent rhyming sounds. Let children play Concentration by matching the words that rhyme.

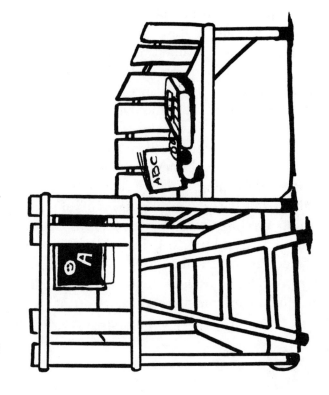

Figure 19

52

- Flannelboard stories: Have children use flannelboard pieces to retell familiar stories.
- Puppets: Provide puppets representing characters in familiar stories so children can present puppet shows. Also provide puppets that do not represent specific stories so children can express personal ideas or create their own stories.
- Using a telephone: Use telephone props and a class telephone book, which has a child's name and phone number on each page. Children can pretend to call each other and talk on the phone.
- Creative drama: Use costumes, masks, props, etc., to represent various stories for children to dramatize.
- Story sequence pictures: Provide sequence pictures or puzzles to represent stories. Children can retell the story as they place the pictures in order.
- Creative stories: Provide pictures to stimulate children when creating their own stories. Provide a tape recorder so children can record and then listen to their stories.

Written Language Activities

- Flannelboard letters/Magnetic letters: Provide letters for children to use. A list of children's names might be posted for children to copy. Also, cards with a simple picture and word written on each can be copied.
- Initial letter sorting: Gather various objects beginning with two or three different consonant sounds. Have children sort them into containers labeled with the initial letter.
- Writing letters: Provide paper, pencils, envelopes, and a list of children's names. Let the children write letters or draw pictures to "mail" to their friends in the class.
- Writing stories: Provide writing materials so children can write their own stories using invented spelling. Interesting objects, such as locust shells or dried seahorses or pictures, will stimulate writing.
- Writing in sand: Provide trays of sand for children to practice writing letters. Sealed zip-lock bags with ketchup or

53

chocolate pudding in them might also be used to write letters. Letters are easily erased after each attempt. Provide letter models.

- Playdough letters: Provide playdough that children can roll and use to form letters. Provide letter models.
- Chalkboard writing: Provide chalkboard, eraser, and chalk for children to write or draw.
- Letter stamps: Provide letter stamps, paper, and an ink pad for children to use. A list of names or simple words might be added for children to copy.
- Typewriter: Provide typewriter or computer for children to use. At first, children might just explore. Later, children might type their own stories using invented spelling.

ART CENTER

Rationale

The art center provides a multitude of opportunities to develop fine motor skills and creative abilities, as well as to promote other areas of development, as children explore and experiment with various art media. When children first begin to manipulate brushes and crayons, they use the materials in an exploratory way. They begin at the scribbling stage, in which they are simply practicing the fine motor skills necessary to control the media. As they gain control, they begin to combine forms and label their creations. They begin to use the materials in a representational manner. With further practice and refinement of eye-hand coordination and pincer grasp skills, children move into a schematic stage of art development. At this point, children begin to use baselines and skylines in their drawings as they begin to see themselves in relation to their world.

Cognitive skills are also developed in the art center. Visual and tactile discriminations are learned through experiences with different media. Thinking processes of inferring, predicting, creating, recalling, and classifying may be involved as children use materials. Art activities should focus on the process rather than the product. In the process approach, children do the thinking and decision making, rather than copying a teacher-made model. The process the child goes through in planning and creating a project is more important than what the finished product looks like.

Language development is stimulated as children verbalize concepts of colors, shape, size, and texture while working with the various materials. Children can dictate statements or stories related to their artwork that the teacher then writes on their paper. All centers lend themselves to informal teacher-child and child-child conversations and the development of beginning readiness skills through the use of symbol charts.

Social and emotional skills are also integrated into the art center. Children can express their own feelings and ideas through their artwork. They develop a sense of pride as they create in their own way. Each child's work is respected and valued. Socially, children learn to share, take turns, and cooperate with others in the use of the various materials.

Aesthetically, children learn about the elements of art and the principles of design. Through their manipulation of various media, they learn about color, shape, line, and texture. They develop an awareness of and an appreciation for art through their own enjoyment. Art becomes a means of aesthetic expression.

Organization

The art center should encompass a fairly large area of the classroom, with room for an easel, work tables, shelves for materials, and a place to dry artwork. The center should be located near a sink for easy cleanup. The floor should be one that is easily cleaned. Plastic dropcloths can be used under the easel, and newspaper can be used to cover tables when messy activities are available. Cleaning materials, such as sponges, paper towels, mop, broom, and dustpan, should be located nearby. Smocks or aprons to protect children's clothing should also be available when messy activities are set up for children to use. Materials should be on low shelves accessible to children. Some materials are always available—scissors, crayons, glue, paper—while others might be only occasionally available. Materials should be arranged on the shelves in an organized manner. Crayons can be sorted according to color and kept in individually color-coded cans. Paper should be separated on the shelf so that children can find the color of their choice. Glue can be kept in plastic squeeze bottles, and scissors should be kept in some type of holder. A simple and inexpensive scissors holder can be made from an upside-down egg carton by punching a hole in the top of each egg cup. Scissors should be the blunt-end or safety type. All materials should be nontoxic and safe for children's use. Figure 20 shows a sketch of an art center arrangement.

Activities

Painting

A variety of painting activities should take place in the art center. Variety is provided through the use of different types of paints, papers, and applicators.

- Easel painting: An easel area should be available where children can use large pieces of newsprint paper and large brushes for the application of tempera paint. Different combinations of colors can be provided each week at the easel. Also, substances such as flour, sugar, salt, and coffee grounds can be added to the paint to produce different textures.
- Foil painting: Provide pieces of foil, small brushes, and small containers of tempera for children to paint with at the table. Adding powdered detergent to the paint will keep the paint from peeling after drying.

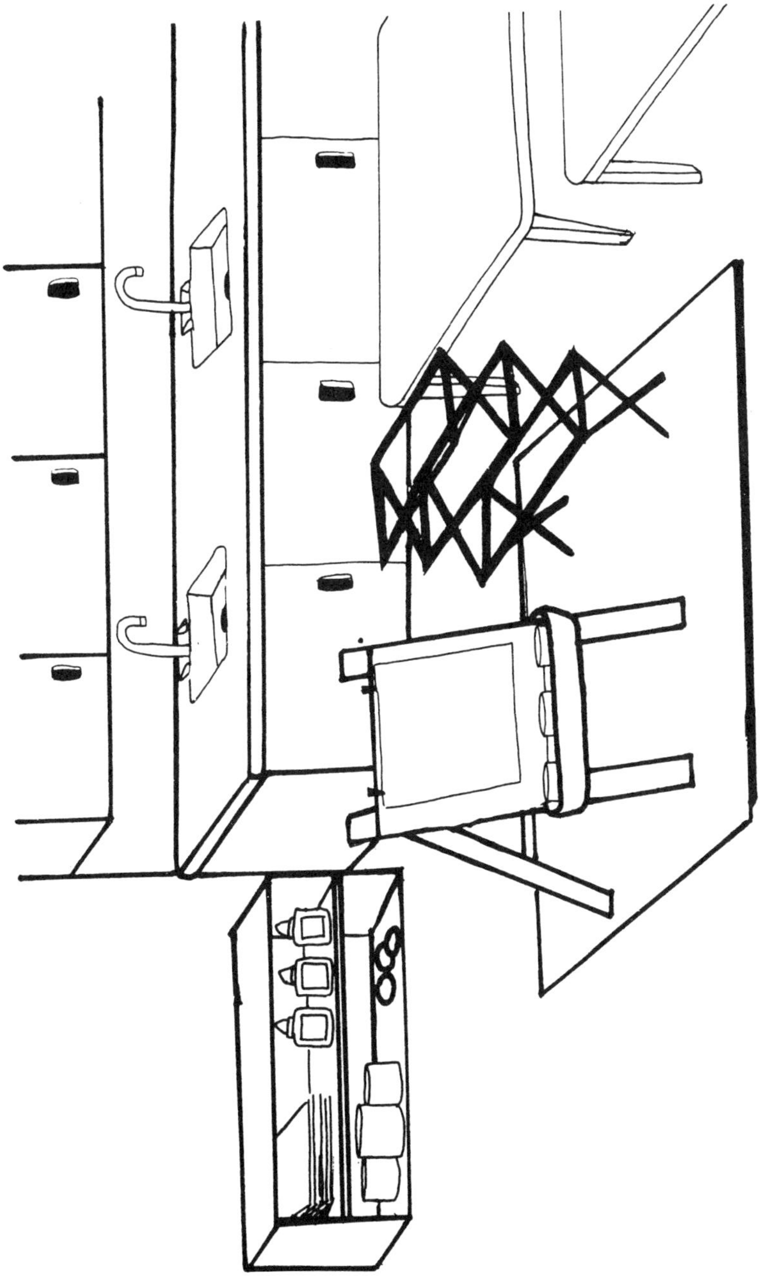

Figure 20

- Drip painting: Place eyedroppers in small containers of tempera paint, and set on a tray on the table. Provide colored construction paper for the children to use as they squeeze the eyedroppers to create their pictures.
- Feather painting: Have the children use feathers instead of brushes to apply the tempera paint to their paper.
- Car track painting: Provide small rubber cars that children can dip into shallow containers of tempera paint and then "drive" on their paper.
- Marble roll: Place marbles in paint containers. Children can place construction paper in a box lid and then drop a marble into the lid. As they move the lid from side to side, the marble paints a picture.
- Fingerpainting: Provide fingerpaint—either commercial or homemade—for children to use. Fingerpaint paper can be provided, or children can paint right on the table top or in a tray. A monoprint might be made by pressing the paper on the child's picture after completion. Other materials that could be used for fingerpainting are pudding, shaving cream, and whipped soap.
- Watercolor paint: The children can use commercial watercolors or water with food coloring added to paint. Paper towels, coffee filters, or other absorbent papers work well.

Modeling Dough

Provide commercial and homemade clays or doughs for children to use. A variety of types of dough will give them different textures to explore. Additional materials can be added to stimulate play: plastic knives, scissors, cookie cutters, rolling pins, and wooden mallets. Kohl (8) provides many homemade recipes that can be used. Here are several examples.

Salty Fundough

Materials

1 cup flour
1 cup water
$1/2$ cup salt
2 t. cream of tartar
2 T. oil
Pan

Process

1. Mix all ingredients in the pan.
2. Cook over low heat until thickened.
3. Cool.
4. Knead.
5. Explore dough freely. (p. 16)

Cornmeal Dough

Materials

$1^1/_2$ cups flour
$1^1/_2$ cups cornmeal
1 cup salt
1 cup water
Bowl

Process

1. Mix all ingredients in the bowl.
2. Add more water to form smooth dough.
3. Model as with any dough. (p. 41)

Oatmeal Dough

Materials

1 cup flour
2 cups oatmeal
1 cup water
Bowl

Process

1. Gradually add water to flour and oatmeal in the bowl.
2. Knead until mixed.
3. Model as with any clay. (p. 42)

Printmaking

A variety of printmaking activities can be provided in the art center. The types of objects available for printing will determine the kinds of experiences children have. When doing printing activities, it is best to use shallow containers with a small amount of paint. A sponge in the bottom of the container will work like an ink pad.

- Cookie cutter prints: Children dip the cookie cutters in paint and then print on paper.
- Sponge prints: Sponges cut into different shapes can be used for printing on paper.
- Vegetable prints: Slice vegetables in half, and let children use them for printing.
- Gadget printing: Let children explore various objects—spool, fork, block, spatula, etc.—through printmaking.
- Rubber stamps: Have children use commercial or home-made rubber stamps to print on paper.

Drawing/Cutting/Gluing

As mentioned earlier, materials for drawing, cutting, and gluing should always be available. Drawing materials could include crayons, water-based markers, and chalk. Scissors can be available for the children's own creative use or for specifically planned activities. Adhesives that can be provided are white glue, white paste, and glue sticks.

- Body outlines: Provide large sheets of butcher paper. As a child lies on the paper, a friend draws around the child's outline. Afterward, the child might color or paint her outline and cut it out if she wishes.
- Chalk drawings: Provide colored chalk, construction paper, and small containers of liquid starch. The children dip the chalk into the starch and then draw.

- Colored glue: Add powdered tempera to white glue to color it, and place the glue in squeeze bottles. Children can squeeze the glue onto paper, foil-covered cardboard pieces, or plastic lids.

- Colored sand: Add powdered tempera to sand or cornmeal to color it. Put the sand or cornmeal in salt shakers, and place it on the table with the glue bottles. Children squeeze glue onto construction paper or paper plates and then sprinkle the colored sand onto the glue.

Collage

Collage making provides children with many different experiences. Various concepts of shape, color, size, and patterns can be developed, depending on the type of materials available.

- Macaroni collage: Color different types of pasta with alcohol and food coloring, and let them dry overnight. Place the paste in the art center with glue and heavy paper or cardboard.

- Tissue paper collage: Use different colors of tissue paper, which might be cut into specific shapes if desired. Children apply the tissue paper to paper by gluing or by brushing on liquid starch and sticking tissue to it.

- Fabric collage: Provide fabric pieces, lace, ribbons, and trims for children to glue onto paper.

- Wallpaper blobs: Let children cut pieces of wallpaper out of sample books and glue them on paper.

- Junk collage: Provide various materials, such as yarn, buttons, toothpicks, cotton balls, styrofoam pieces, craft sticks, and straws, for children to use in their collage.

- Magazine collage: Let children cut pictures out of magazines or catalogs to glue on their collage. Collages can have a specific theme—red pictures, foods, toys, pictures of various feelings, etc.

TABLE GAMES CENTER

Rationale

In the table games center, the children have the opportunity to work with small manipulative activities either individually or with a friend. A variety of games provides for the development of perceptual, conceptual, and fine motor skills. Cognitive skills are developed as children manipulate pieces of different shapes, colors, and sizes. Children learn to discriminate these various attributes and to sort, classify, and sequence objects according to these attributes.

Language skills are enhanced as they learn the vocabulary related to the various concepts presented in the table games center. In addition to the concepts described above, children learn concepts of quantity. They also develop language abilities as they interact informally with other children and the teacher—asking questions and engaging in conversations.

Fine motor skills are developed through stringing beads, placing pegs in a pegboard, using construction games, making puzzles, and manipulating small pieces of games. Activities that develop such self-help skills as lacing, buttoning, tying, and zipping can also be used in the table games center.

Emotionally, children learn to work independently and to feel a sense of pride and accomplishment when they complete a puzzle or game. Social skills of sharing and taking turns are also developed.

Aesthetically, children learn about the art elements of line, color, shape, and texture as they explore objects. Children might create patterns or designs through the use of blocks, parquetry, bead stringing, or pegboards.

Organization

The table games area needs enough shelf space to hold a

variety of games each week, about 10–15. The games could be commercial learning games or teacher-made games that vary in level of difficulty. Most games should allow the child to work individually, but some simple cooperative games might be included. Late in the kindergarten year, as egocentrism diminishes in five-year-olds, children become better able to participate in cooperative games. They begin to understand the rules, but taking turns in games is still a major learning for these children.

Space to play the games can be provided in two different ways. You can provide tables and chairs where the children sit and use the games, or you might want to provide an open carpeted area where the children sit on the floor and work with the games. One way to simplify the set-up of table games is to place each game on an individual tray. Different parts of the game can be organized and arranged on the tray. For example, the pegboards, a bowl containing the pegs, and a set of pattern cards can be placed on the tray beside each other. This helps to keep all the pieces of one game together. Children take the whole tray from the shelf to work with it and then return it. Some games that have many large pieces, such as construction games, can be placed in large plastic tubs and set on the shelf. Providing trays for puzzles keeps small pieces in a confined area. Some teachers place a stack of trays in this center for children's use, rather than placing each game on a tray. In our kindergarten classroom, the teacher divides the table games center into two separate areas—table games and mathematics. In the math area, a table, chairs, and a shelf containing only mathematics-related games are provided. The table games area contains other types of manipulative games. Figure 21 shows a sketch of a table game center arrangement.

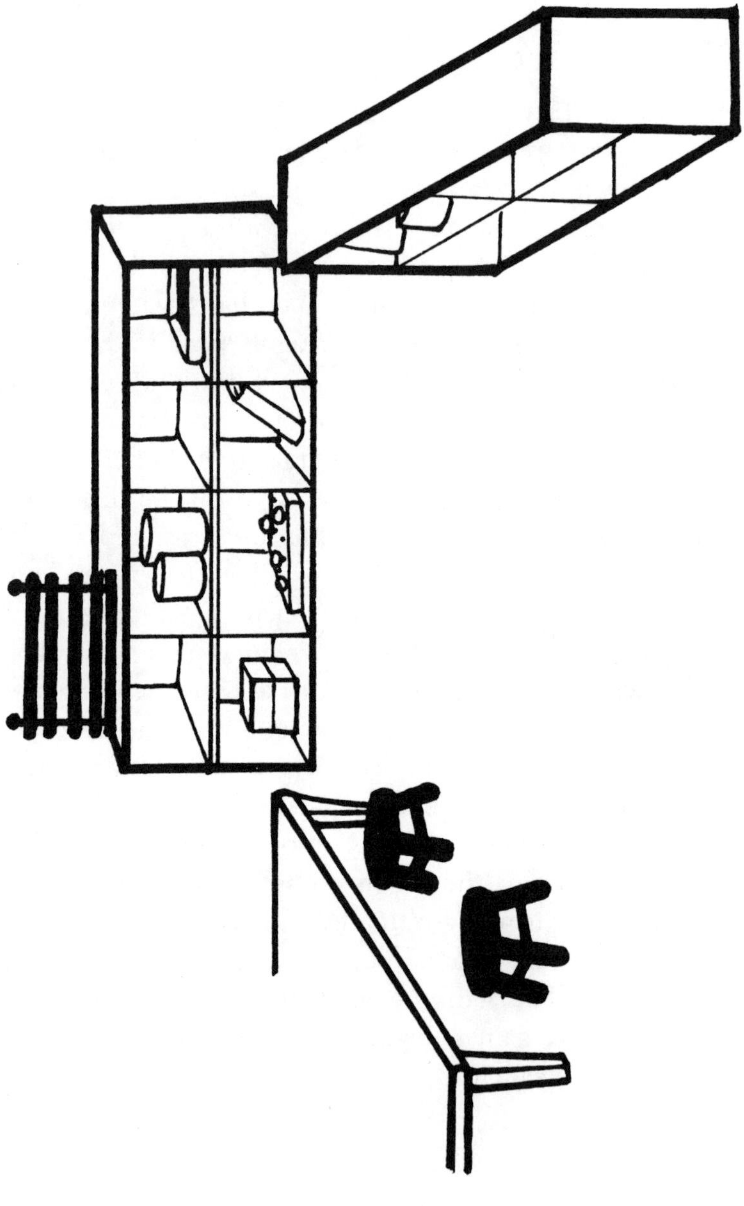

Figure 21

Activities

Manipulative Games

- Puzzles: A variety of puzzles (6–10) should be available each week. The puzzles should represent different levels of difficulty. Puzzles should be kept in a puzzle rack.
- Sewing cards: Provide sewing cards and laces for children to use. Homemade cards can be made by punching holes around the edges of greeting cards.
- Construction toys: Commercial construction toys, such as Legos, Tinkertoys, and Construx, and table blocks should be provided.
- Pegboards: Provide various sizes of pegboards and pegs for children to manipulate. Pattern cards could be used as models for children to copy.

Discrimination Games

- Tactile match: Use tongue depressors covered on one side with various fabric textures or different grades of sandpaper for children to match.
- Visual discrimination: Make cards with fabric swatches, wallpaper samples, pictures, or stickers for children to match.

Ordering Games

- Size sequencing: Have children sequence wooden rods from short to long or pictures of objects from small to large. Provide double sets of sequence pictures for children to separate and match, such as the smallest plant to the smallest flower pot and increasing in size to the largest plant and the largest flower pot.
- Sequencing pictures: Provide pictures that illustrate a sequence of events, such as a plant growing or a chick hatching out of an egg, for children to place in order from first to last.

- Light-to-dark sequence: Have children place paint samples in order from light to dark for various colors.
- Stringing beads: Provide beads of various shapes or colors and laces for stringing. Provide pattern cards for children to follow in sequencing the beads.

Sorting/Classifying Games

- Shape sorting: Use attribute blocks or parquetry pieces for children to sort into containers identified by the various shapes.
- Design pattern sorting: Have children sort fabric swatches into containers representing stripes, prints, solids, plaids, and polka dots.
- Button sorting: Provide a container of buttons of various types. Let children sort them into a tray or egg carton based on attributes of color, size, or number of holes.

Mathematics Games

- Set matching: Have children match objects in one-to-one correspondence, such as placing one straw in a cup with one dot on it, two straws in a cup with two dots, etc.
- Numeral/set matching: Have children match the correct number of objects to the numeral, such as clipping three clothespins to the card with the numeral 3 or counting beads and placing an amount in the cup of an egg carton that matches the numeral written inside the cup.
- Pie pan fractions: Cut at least four colored poster board circles about 10 inches in diameter. Cut one of the circles in half, one in thirds, one in fourths, and one in sixths. Let children put them together to make wholes.

Cooperative Games

- Card games: Provide commercial or homemade card games that require children to match pairs.
- Dominoes: Provide dominoes that require number, color, shape, or picture matching.

- Board games: Use simple trail games for children to roll dice, use spinners, or select cards to designate moves.
- Lotto games: Use game boards, markers, and cards that represent colors, shapes, numbers, letters, or pictures.

DISCOVERY CENTER

Rationale

The discovery center is an area in the classroom where children can participate in a variety of activities that stimulate curiosity, exploration, and problem solving. This center is especially well suited to the development of mathematics and science concepts. Here children can develop physical knowledge as they work with the objects and logical-mathematical knowledge as they think about the logical relationships within and among objects.

Children develop sensory skills and concepts of sight, sound, taste, touch, and smell as they match objects that are alike or sort those that are different. Thinking and reasoning skills are stimulated through the many discovery activities. Children could order objects by height or weight. Classification activities could include sorting objects by shape, color, size, material, or function. Children make inferences and predictions as they use magnets or engage in water-play activities. New vocabulary develops related to the various activities. Such concepts as rough/smooth, short/tall, sweet/sour, more/less, and soft/hard are some of the many that may be learned.

Fine motor skills are developed as children pour water, sand, and rice. Also, children develop pincer control as they use utensils in cooking activities and manipulate small objects.

Social-emotional skills develop as children share and cooperate with materials. Compassion and caring skills are encouraged as children learn responsibility for plants and animals.

Aesthetic concepts of line, shape, symmetry, balance, and design can be stimulated as children observe and learn about the properties of objects.

Organization

The discovery center should have things for the children to "do." It is not a center where children just look at objects. Our teachers use a sand and water table in the discovery center. Here various materials —rice, beans, cornmeal, sawdust, mud—can be placed in the table for children to explore, measure, and pour. The table helps to contain the materials with a minimum of mess. Plastic tubs or dishpans can be used instead. A broom, dustpan, or mop should be located nearby. If plastic tubs of water are set on a table, towels can be spread on the table to absorb spills. Sand and water activities are usually open-ended—that is, children can freely explore and manipulate materials with no definite or specified end to the activity. Some discovery activities have a more specific purpose, such as sensory discrimination, sequencing, and classification activities. However, when children first begin, they can use the materials in an exploratory fashion. Later, they can use them for the purpose intended—to match, sequence, or sort. The complexity level of the activity can be increased as needed. For example, in using an activity such as "sink and float," children might at first simply explore the water and the objects. Next, children might be able to test the objects and sort them appropriately into containers, as shown in Figure 22. Later, children might be able to use a prediction chart (Figure 23) on which they record whether or not they think the object will sink or float before testing the object. Children can then test the objects and check their predictions.

Another type of activity that we do in discovery is cooking. Recipes that children can prepare individually with a minimum of teacher supervision work well in the discovery center. There are many simple recipes that do not require

Figure 22

Float   Sink

Figure 23

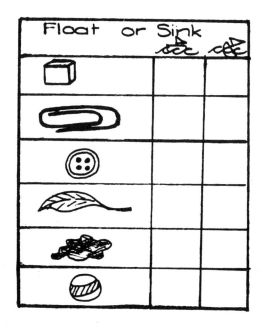

cooking. If heating utensils are used, then an adult must be present to supervise and assist.

The discovery center can house plants and animals for the children to observe. In addition to caring for them, the children can also record information about them, such as the amount of food given to the gerbil each day, the amount of water used for the plant, or the amount the plant has grown. Figure 24 shows a sketch of a discovery center.

Activities

Sand/Water Activities

- Measuring: Provide water, sand, or other materials along with measuring cups and containers of various sizes for children to measure and pour.
- Blowing bubbles: Add liquid soap to the water and provide straws for children to blow bubbles.
- Goop: Add water to cornstarch and let children explore with their hands.

Sensory Activities

- Tactile match: Place simple objects, such as a ball, block, and spoon, in a feel box. Have children explore and match these to pictures of objects.
- Listening cans: Place different objects or substances, such as sand, paper clips, rocks, and marbles, in soft drink cans, and tape over the openings. Have two cans of each for children to shake and match.
- Tasting: Have small pieces of fruit for children to taste and match to pictures.

Ordering/Sequencing Activities

- Size sequence: Have dowel rods of different lengths for children to sequence from shortest to longest.

Figure 24

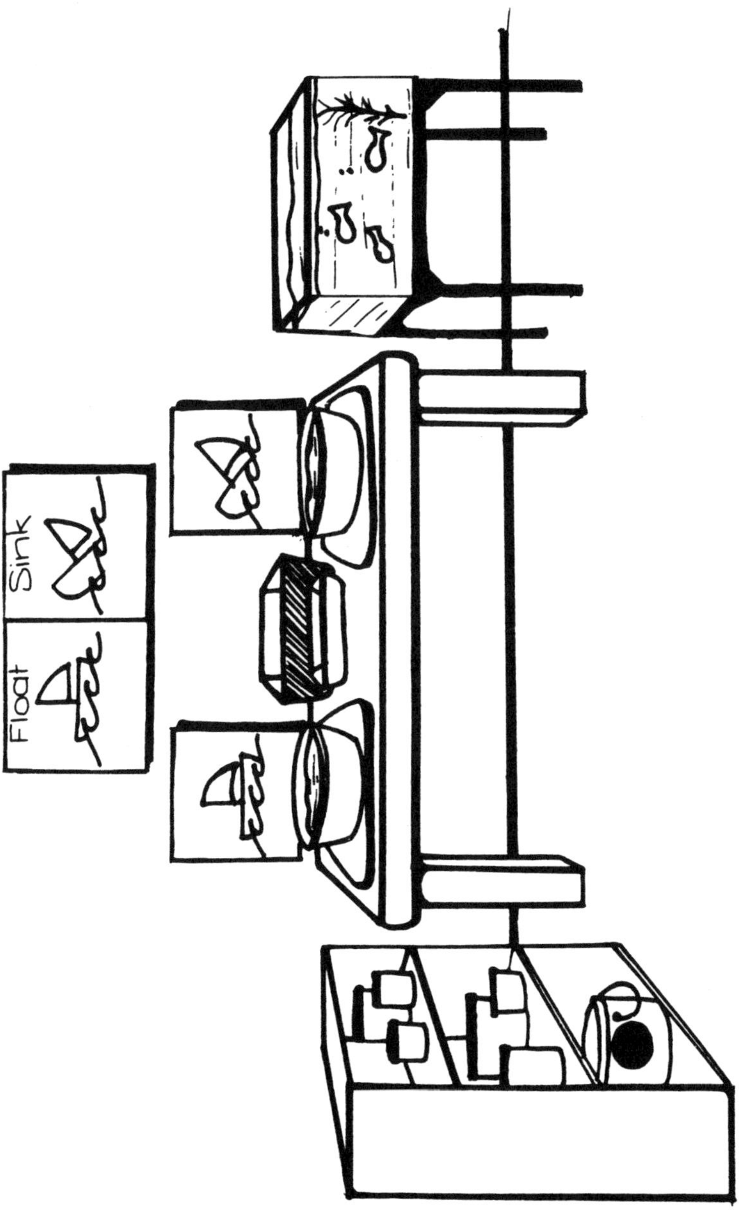

Float | Sink

- Weight cans: Fill soft drink cans with varying amounts of plaster. Let them dry, and cover the openings. Have children order them from lightest to heaviest.

Sorting/Classification Activities

- Heavy/light: Use a balance scale with an object taped on one side. Provide other objects for children to weigh on other side. Children sort objects that are heavier or lighter than the taped object.
- Small/medium/large: Have several objects in three sizes, such as three sizes of balls, pencils, and blocks. Have children sort these into containers according to size.
- Food/clothing/toys: Provide cards with pictures of food, clothing, and toys. Have children sort them into containers marked with a picture of each.

Prediction Activities

- Attract/repel: Provide objects and magnets for children to explore. Provide a prediction chart for children to record their predictions before testing the objects.
- How many? Provide containers of several different sizes and small objects, such as marbles. Children predict or estimate how many marbles it will take to fill each container. They then check their predictions.

Measuring Activities

- Height chart: Provide a height chart for children to mark each other's height and compare.
- Measuring length: Provide small objects for children to measure—a block, pencil, and piece of paper. Have children measure with paper clips or strips of yarn.

Cooking Activities

- Stuffed celery: Have children cut celery stalks into smaller pieces and spread them with cream cheese.

- Peanut butter crackers: Have children spread peanut butter on crackers and place raisins on top.
- Making butter: Have children pour a small amount of whipping cream into a baby food jar and shake. After a few minutes, spread the butter on crackers.

DRAMATIC PLAY CENTER

Rationale

The dramatic play center is an area of the classroom where children can engage in role-playing activities. During the preoperational stage of cognitive development, children begin to use symbols, and through their pretend play, they practice and improve their symbolization skills. Rather than verbally recalling events, as adults do, children recall what has happened by dramatizing previous events. They rethink through pretend play. Smilansky (16) identified six play elements that are essential to well-developed sociodramtic play:

1. *Imitative role play.* The child undertakes a make-believe role and expresses it in imitative action and/or verbalizations.
2. *Make-believe in regard to objects.* Movements or verbal declarations are substituted for real objects.
3. *Make-believe in regard to actions and situations.* Verbal descriptions are substituted for actions and situations.
4. *Persistence.* The child persists in a play episode for at least 10 minutes.
5. *Interaction.* There are at least two players interacting in the framework of the play episode.
6. *Verbal communication.* There is some verbal interaction related to the play episode.

One developmental area that receives a major emphasis in the dramatic play center is language. Through their role play, children practice using language in a variety of situations—

talking on the telephone, ordering a hamburger, selling shoes, and talking to the doctor about an injury. They learn new vocabulary as they use the objects and reenact their experiences associated with the dramatic play situations. They practice conversational skills and learn to listen and exchange information with others. Literacy skills are stimulated as print—store signs, phone books, appointment books, grocery ads, magazines, price tags, and writing materials—is incorporated into the dramatic play area.

Cognitive skills are developed as children sequence events in the role-play situation, such as the steps in making a pizza. Children classify objects when they sort items in a clothing store or foods in a grocery store. Number skills are developed as children count objects and use play money in their activities.

Physical development is enhanced through the use of activities that require fine motor manipulation. Children develop skills in using tools in the garage area or utensils in the bakery center. Self-help skills of buttoning, zipping, and tying are practiced as children put on clothing or costumes. Pincer control is developed through the manipulation of small objects.

The dramatic play center is specifically useful in developing social skills. By pretending to be another person, children learn social role-taking skills. Their egocentric viewpoint lessens when they begin to see situations from another person's point of view. Children also learn to work cooperatively as roles are divided among the different players, such as the doctor, nurse, patient, and receptionist. Emotionally, the dramatic play center allows children to reenact situations that might be frightening, such as going to the doctor or the hospital, in a safe play situation. This allows children an outlet to express and deal with their fears.

In the area of aesthetic development, the dramatic play center is well suited to the development of the dramatic arts. Children use imitative actions and sounds. They also develop skill in using their body and voice in an expressive manner.

Organization

The dramatic play center should be located in a large area of the classroom. This allows adequate space to set up a variety of areas, such as two rooms of a home or a waiting room and an examination room for the doctor's office. Dramatic play should begin with familiar themes. A home arrangement allows children to play out the familiar roles of family. The home center can be varied by adding props for dishwashing, washing clothes, or washing babies. As children's play develops, other familiar situations, such as the doctor's office and the grocery store, work well. Children need real experiences before using symbolic play; therefore, field trips are a useful way to expose children to the objects and activities that are related to the dramatic play theme. When it is not possible to take a trip, a resource guest might be able to come to the classroom to talk about his work. Books should also be used to provide additional information about various situations. Related pictures that help to stimulate play can be posted in the center.

The props provided in the dramatic play center stimulate activity on the part of the child. In the beginning, children need realistic props—a real telephone or a toy phone that looks realistic. Later, children can move to more representational objects. As children's fantasy play skills improve, they will need fewer objects to support their play. Also, they will be able to construct their own props from materials provided. Simple costumes can be made by using pillow cases. Cut holes at the top and sides for the child's head and arms. Permanent markers can be used to draw a uniform or other pattern on the case. Props for the different dramatic play themes can be organized into prop boxes. A large box could be labeled for the baker. In it can be kept aprons, hats, cookie cutters, rolling pins, pans, bowls, and utensils. When the teacher wants to set up the bakery, she can take out the box and have most of the props that will be needed. At the end of a week or two, the items can then be packed away in the box and stored easily for future use. Many items can be easily collected for prop boxes. Parents might be able to donate items related to the home or their work. Inexpensive items can be purchased at garage sales. Also, many businesses will donate items to the school. Sketches of a dramatic play home center (Figure 25) and a doctor's office (Figure 26) follow.

Activities

- Home: Arrange kitchen and bedroom areas. Provide child-size table, chairs, sink, refrigerator, stove, doll bed, and dresser. Add dolls (multiethnic), clothes, food props, a telephone, and dishes.

- Grocery store: Arrange a checkout stand and shelves for foods. Provide empty food boxes and cans, plastic fruits and vegetables, shopping baskets, sacks, a cash register, money, clothes, purses, and wallets.

- Doctor's office: Arrange a waiting room, receptionist desk, and an examination area. Provide doctors' and nurses' uniforms and bags, syringes, gloves, masks, white sheet, bandages, and magazines.

- Restaurant: Arrange seating and kitchen areas. Provide props for various types of eating places—pizza, hamburger, chicken, Italian, Chinese, etc. For example, pizza ingredients can be cut out of felt for children to assemble. Add cups, plates, napkins, menus, order pads, money, and a cash register.

- Pet store: Arrange an area for pet cages and a checkout counter. Provide stuffed animals (dogs, cats, rabbits, birds, fish), boxes for cages, pet supplies, pet food containers, leashes, collars, brushes, a cash register, and money.

- Shoe store: Arrange shelves to display shoes and a checkout area. Provide different-sized shoes for men, women, boys, and girls; socks; hose; purses; a foot measurement device; a cash register; shoe boxes; and money.

Figure 25

Figure 26

- Circus: Arrange a ticket counter, a seating area, and a performance area. Provide a cash register, tickets, a balance beam, a trampoline, stilts, a tumbling mat, costumes, and clown makeup.
- Garage/fix-it shop: Arrange a work area with a table and shelves. Provide a variety of tools, old car parts, and broken appliances for children to "repair."
- Flower shop: Arrange an order counter and a work area. Provide a sand table with a container for potting flowers. Real or plastic flowers could be used. Florists will often donate old flowers. Add ribbons, a cash register, order forms, and cards.
- Post office: Arrange a writing area, a postal counter, and a mailbox area. Provide paper, markers, pencils, and envelopes for children to write letters. Add uniforms and mailbags for postal workers to take mail and sort it into mailboxes.

BLOCKS CENTER

Rationale

The primary purpose of the blocks center is to engage the children in building activities. Children go through seven stages in block building. Very young children or children who have not had experiences with blocks may first carry the blocks or place them in a pile without actually building. The second stage is when children begin to stack the blocks in rows. Third, the children begin to bridge the space between two blocks. Fourth, the children form enclosures by completely enclosing a space with blocks. In the fifth stage, children begin to form decorative patterns with the blocks, using the skills practiced in the earlier stages. Next, children begin to build representationally and to label or name their buildings. Finally, children will begin to construct actual buildings with which they have had experience (4).

Building with blocks can stimulate the development of skills in all areas of the curriculum. Children develop cognitive skills of seriation and classification as they observe and manipulate blocks of different sizes and shapes. Number concepts of quantity and whole-part relationships can be learned. Children also develop positional concepts and spatial awareness as they move themselves or props around the block structures.

Oral language skills are stimulated as children hear and verbalize labels for the many concepts presented in the block center. Literacy skills may be enhanced as written labels and charts are used in the block center. Paper and writing utensils might be provided for children to use to label their own buildings.

Both gross motor and fine motor skills are also practiced in the block center. Children may be using the gross motor skills of bending, pushing, and pulling as they manipulate the blocks and props. Fine motor skills are used as children place and align blocks carefully while building.

The blocks center provides a means of self-expression as children create their own structures or reconstruct their own experiences. Social skills are enhanced as children learn to share and take turns with materials and to work cooperatively to build larger structures.

Aesthetic design principles are stimulated as children build, using symmetrical and repetitive patterns. Children can also use creative dramatizations in acting out situations in the blocks center.

Organization

The blocks center should be located in a large, open area of the classroom. There should be adequate space for children to build individually without interfering in each other's work. A hard-nap carpet should be provided to muffle the sound of falling blocks. Plenty of shelf space should be provided so that the various shapes and sizes of blocks can be separated for easy storage

80

and cleanup. Outlines of the blocks should be drawn on the shelves so that children will know where to place blocks after use.

Two types of blocks are appropriate for young children. Unit blocks are small blocks originally designed by Caroline Pratt (4). Many of the blocks are multiples or fractional parts of the basic unit. Additional decorative shapes are also available. Hollow blocks are the second type. These blocks are large and come in fewer sizes and shapes. Separate shelves should be provided for each type of blocks. Unit blocks and hollow blocks are not usually combined because they lead to different kinds of play. With the hollow blocks, children can build a structure and then actually get inside for role-playing activities, such as building a boat and then pretending to use it on a lake to go fishing. With the unit blocks, children are manipulating small props and then projecting themselves into the play mentally. For example, a child may build a dock area and pretend to go fishing in a small plastic boat that she is manipulating. Our teachers put a "closed" sign (Figure 18) on the type of blocks that are not to be played with each week.

Props can be added to the blocks center to stimulate play. However, at the beginning of the year, no props should be provided so that children can practice building skills, rather than just playing with the props. After children's skills have improved, add props such as transportation toys, rubber animal figures, people figures, and street signs. Props should be appropriately sized to the size of the blocks—small props with the unit blocks and large props with the hollow blocks. Figure 27 shows a sketch of a blocks center.

Because the blocks center requires more time for cleanup, children in this area should begin cleaning up before the children in other centers do. Also, encourage children to take out blocks only as they need them and to clean up their blocks before they leave the center. If a large number of blocks are out at cleanup time, children from other areas of the classroom can be recruited to assist.

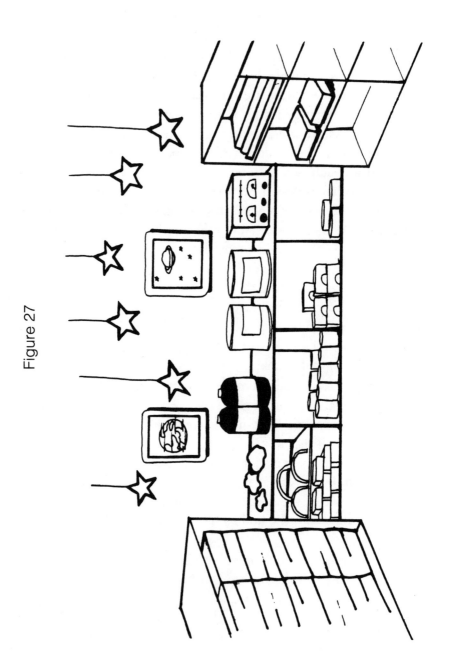

Figure 27

Activities

Unit Blocks

- Building roads: Provide small cars, street signs, and pictures of streets. Have children construct roads.
- Building bridges: Provide small boats, pieces of blue vinyl to represent bodies of water, and pictures of bridges. Have children build bridges over the water.
- Blueprint building: Draw block structure patterns on poster board, and post them in the center for children to copy.
- Body shape: Have one child lie down on the floor while another child uses blocks to outline his body.
- Building houses: Provide dollhouse furniture and pictures of rooms. Have children build houses and arrange the furniture.
- Zoo: Provide rubber zoo animals and pictures. Let children build areas for the animals.
- Farm: Provide rubber farm animals and pictures. Let children build a barn and fences for a farm.
- Airport: Provide small planes and pictures. Have children build an airport terminal and runways.
- Homes: Provide pictures of different types of homes—log cabins, apartment buildings, brick houses, etc. Have children build homes.
- Doghouses: Provide three sizes of stuffed dogs, bowls, and dog bones. Have children build houses appropriately sized to fit the dogs.

Hollow Blocks

- Fishing: Provide wooden oars, fishing poles, hats, a steering wheel, and pictures of boats. Let children build their own boat.
- Space travel: Provide space pictures, earphones, and homemade space helmets and uniforms. Have children build a spaceship.
- Bus/train: Provide pictures, chairs for seats, tickets, and a driver or conductor hat. Let children build a bus or a train.

MUSIC CENTER

Rationale

The music center provides opportunities for children to participate in activities involving singing, instruments, and movement or dance. Children develop an aesthetic appreciation for various types of music and an awareness of music elements such as rhythm, tempo, and pitch. They may be involved in creative expression as they move to the music.

Dance and movement activities enhance the development of many motor skills. Children may develop locomotor skills as they walk, jump, hop, skip, or gallop around the center to the beat of the music. Nonlocomotor skills of bending, twisting, stretching, and spinning are developed as children use free expression when listening to music. Manipulative skills can be used as children manipulate props or instruments in the music center.

The music center also stimulates language skills. Children develop listening skills as they listen to directions on a record or listen to various instruments and types of music. Speaking skills are developed as children sing songs and practice various language structures and patterns, as well as when they have informal conversations. Children also learn language concepts specific to the music center. Literacy skills can be stimulated through the use of symbol charts, song cards, and color-coded song charts.

Cognitively, children develop discrimination and conceptual skills as they identify similarities and differences in high and low, loud and soft, and fast and slow. They could be involved in sequencing the notes of a song as they play a xylophone or in repeating a pattern as they clap rhythms.

The music center also enhances social-emotional skills. As children dance to the music, they are able to express their own ideas and feelings. They learn to share materials and to work cooperatively as they take on different roles to dramatize a song.

Organization

The music center should be large enough that children have room to move. A table or shelf is needed on which to place instruments or props and a tape recorder or record player. The record player or tape recorder should be made self-directing. Use colored tape for marking, such as red tape on the "stop" button, green for "go," and yellow for "rewind." Tape can also be used to indicate the volume level. Tapes and records can be coded to their covers or cases by symbols. If you put, for example, a blue square on the record and on the cover, children can easily return the record to its correct place.

For singing activities, song cards (Figure 28) can be made and placed in the center. This enables children to pick their favorite songs to sing on their own or with a friend. Songs should be short and repetitious and have a limited vocal range. For very young children or children with limited singing experience, begin with a six-note range. Props related to songs can be provided so children can dramatize songs as they sing them.

Children enjoy music of all types, so a variety of music experiences should be provided for children's listening. As children hear classical, jazz, pop, and country music, they develop an awareness and appreciation of music styles. Also, records of music from other countries and cultures can be used.

When instruments are added to the music center, they should have a specific purpose. Instruments are not used just to make "noise," but rather to enhance the activity. Instruments should be in good condition, and rules for how to use instruments appropriately should be previewed ahead of time. Instruments may be hung on a pegboard or placed on a shelf.

Movement and dance activities should be of two types: rhythmic and creative. In rhythmic activities, the emphasis is on keeping the beat of the music. In creative activities, the emphasis is on the child's free expression to the music. Limits can be set on the area for movement by using carpet or by marking an area on

Figure 28

the floor with tape. A diagram of a music center is shown in Figure 29.

Activities

Singing

- Dramatizing a song: Provide props so children can dramatize the song as they sing. For example, with the song "Miss Polly Had a Dolly," provide a doll, telephone, doctor's bag, and hat.
- Taping songs: Provide song cards and a tape recorder. Let children choose and sing their favorite songs. They can record them and then listen to themselves.
- Talent show: Provide a stage area and chairs for the audience. Microphones can be made by covering cardboard tubes with foil. Add costumes and instruments for children to use as they perform.

Listening

- Drawing to music: Provide tapes of different types of music, paper, and crayons. As children listen to the music, they can draw a picture expressing their feelings.
- Reproducing rhythm patterns: Provide a tape of various rhythm patterns for children to reproduce by clapping.

Instruments

- Instrument identification game: Set up the music center with two chairs and tables separated by a divider. On one side of the divider, place several rhythm instruments on the table. On the other side, place pictures of the instruments. As the child on one side plays an instrument, the child on the other side holds up the picture of the identified instrument.
- Color-coded instruments: Color-code the notes of a xylophone or other instrument. Make a symbol chart showing the sequence of colored dots that represents a simple song. Children can follow the sequence to play the song on the xylophone.

Figure 29

Rhythmic Movement

- Marching: Provide a tape of marching music. Add such props as batons, flags, or instruments for children to use as they march to the music.
- Riding horses: Provide appropriate western-style music and stick horses. Children can ride the horses to the beat of the music.
- Bouncing balls: Provide music with a strong rhythmic beat. Have children bounce or dribble a ball to the beat of the music.

Creative Movement

- Dancing with scarves: Provide scarves or streamers for children to use creatively as they move and dance to expressive music.
- Dance costumes: Provide dance costumes for children to wear as they dance, such as grass skirts and leis for hula dancing, and music that is appropriate for the costumes.

CONSTRUCTION CENTER

Rationale

The construction center allows children the opportunity to reconstruct their world. When children first begin to work in the construction center, they often will use the materials in an exploratory manner and practice hammering and sawing skills. Later, they will begin to label their constructions and to build actual objects.

Many motor skills are developed through children's work in the construction center. Children use gross motor skills as they push and pull the saw and manipulative skills as they use hammers, screwdrivers, and other tools. Fine motor skills are developed as children use a pincer grasp when handling nails and small objects and also manipulative tools and scissors.

Language skills are enhanced as children label the concepts of texture, color, shape, size, and quantity while working with the available materials. Symbol charts stimulate print awareness, and materials for labeling creations can be provided.

Cognitively, children learn to discriminate and classify the various types of materials used based on visual, textural, functional, or property characteristics. They might have to plan and sequence the steps to complete a project.

As children work in the construction center, various social and emotional skills will be used. Children might have to take turns and share tools and materials. They might work cooperatively to build something together. Also, children learn to follow rules of safety for themselves and others.

Aesthetically, children learn about the design concepts of symmetry and balance and the art principles of color, line, form, and texture. They experiment with a variety of media as they create in the construction center.

Organization

The construction center includes two types of activities. Woodworking activities use tools, such as hammers, saws, a vise, screwdrivers, nails, and screws. The other type of activity is constructive art, in which glue and other materials are used to build structures with wood, boxes, styrofoam, paper tubes, and other three-dimensional materials. Collage materials and paint may be added to either woodworking or constructive art activities. No matter which type of activity is planned for the construction center, the focus should be on the creative process and not on just copying a teacher-made project, as was discussed with regard to the art center.

For woodworking activities, real tools of good quality should be used. Tools should be outlined on a tray or hung on a pegboard and kept in good condition. Tools should be introduced to the children slowly, and time should be provided for children to practice and gain control in using the tools. For example, when introducing the hammer, discuss safety rules for its use. Provide blocks of wood with nails partially hammered in for children to finish hammering. This will help children learn to control the hammer before actually holding the nails themselves. Nails with large heads work best. Later, children can practice hammering nails into styrofoam and then into soft wood. When children saw, spray the saw with WD-40 to make it move more easily through the wood. Safety glasses should be used to help prevent accidents.

Many materials used in the construction center can be collected easily and inexpensively. Some lumber companies, frame shops, and craft stores will donate scrap pieces of wood for schools to use. Parents might also be able to collect "junk," such as empty food boxes, paper towel tubes, styrofoam packing pieces, cardboard, plastic bottles, plastic milk jug lids, etc. Collage materials that are used in the art center may also be used in the construction center to decorate constructions. A sketch of a construction center is shown in Figure 30.

Activities

Woodworking

- Nailing logs: When children are first hammering into wood, provide a section of a log for children to use to practice hammering nails.
- Nailing shapes: Draw shapes onto blocks of wood with a marker and have children nail around the shapes. Children can draw their own design or write their name to use for nailing.
- Build a body: Provide blocks of wood for the trunk of the body. Provide circular pieces of construction paper and markers for children to draw their faces. Also, provide construction paper cutouts for legs and arms. Have children nail the body together.

Figure 30

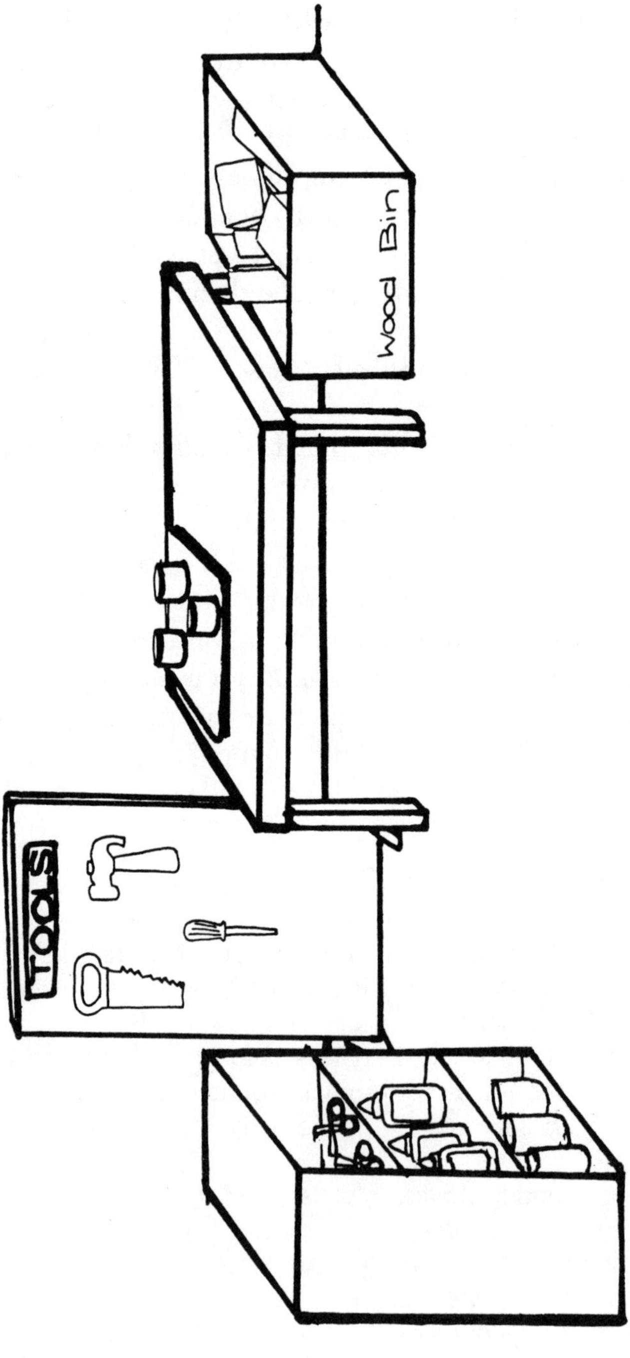

TOOLS

Wood Bin

- Building houses: Provide wood, hammers, nails, paint, and pictures of houses. Let children build and paint a house of their own design.
- Building vehicles: Provide rectangular blocks of wood and circular objects, such as bottle caps or plastic milk jug lids. Add pictures of cars, trucks, and trains. Let children hammer pieces together to build vehicles.
- Making puzzles: Provide pieces of plywood, markers, and saws. Let children draw a picture on the wood and then cut it into pieces to make a puzzle.

Constructive Art

- Pets: Post pictures of pets in the center. Provide such materials as paper towel tubes, pipe cleaners, construction paper, scissors, glue, and markers for children to create their own pet.
- Choose and create: Specify a certain quantity of each material for children to use to create anything they want. For example, have them use one egg carton, two paper tubes, four straws, and four pieces of yarn to create something.
- Box sculpture: Provide small cardboard boxes in a variety of shapes and sizes, glue, and paint. Let children glue together a structure and then paint it.
- Styrofoam sculpture: Provide styrofoam pieces, both large sections and small packing pieces. Allow children to make a sculpture using glue, toothpicks, or pipe cleaners to connect the styrofoam.
- Collage: Provide pieces of wood to serve as the base. Let children glue various collage materials—yarn, straws, styrofoam, buttons, toothpicks, etc.—to make their designs.

GROSS MOTOR CENTER

Rationale

The gross motor center provides an opportunity for children to practice large muscle skills. Young children need to be able to move and be active throughout the day. While children have opportunities for large muscle play outside, we also set aside an area in the classroom. This provides an area where children can be very physically active in a constructive and appropriate manner.

The emphasis in the gross motor center is on the development of large muscle skills. Children develop the locomotor skills of crawling, jumping, hopping, skipping, and galloping and the nonlocomotor skills of bending, stretching, twisting, spinning, pushing, and pulling. The perceptual-motor skills of spatial awareness, balance, and eye-hand coordination are also used as children move their bodies and objects through space.

Social skills are learned as children take turns playing cooperative games, such as hopscotch and bowling. Emotionally, children feel pride in themselves as they master control of their body and learn new skills.

Children develop language concepts related to movement and spatial direction such as *under, over, around, through, forward,* and *backward.* Symbol charts can be used to give directions, and recording charts give children an opportunity to write down their scores.

Cognitive skills are used as children count the number of jumping jacks they do or add their points in bowling. They can use sequencing skills as they move through an obstacle course. They also develop physical knowledge as they act on objects, such as throwing a beanbag or hitting a suspended yarn ball.

Aesthetic activity can occur as children use imitative movements. Children also learn to use their body expressively as they gain body awareness and control.

Organization

Because the gross motor center involves large muscle activity, a fairly large open area must be provided. If adequate space is not available in the classroom, sometimes a hallway outside the classroom can be used. The teacher can supervise the children by opening the doorway to the hall. Whether inside the classroom or in the hallway, the boundaries of the gross motor center should be clearly marked using tape or dividers to prevent the activity from disrupting others. Many appropriate and inexpensive materials can be provided for the gross motor center. Foam balls and yarn balls allow opportunities for many ball activities inside without concern for the balls bouncing into other areas. Paddles or racquets can be made by bending a clothes hanger into a diamond shape and covering it with a hosiery leg. The excess hosiery can be wrapped around the hooked end of the hanger to ensure safety and to provide a handle. A 2 × 4 board can be mounted at the ends to provide a homemade balance beam, and an old mattress can serve as a tumbling mat.

Because of the space requirements in the gross motor center, only one activity might be provided in the center each week. A sketch of a gross motor center is shown in Figure 31.

Activities

- Animal spinner: Make a spinner game with pictures of animals such as a kangaroo, a frog, a snake, a rabbit, and a duck. Tape a path on floor. Children spin and move around the path like that animal.

- Obstacle course: Set up a course with such equipment as a balance beam, a tunnel, stair steps, cone markers, and small sawhorses. Tape arrows on the floor to show direction. Allow children to move over, around, under, and through the equipment.

- Beanbag toss: Provide several beanbags and a target for children to use. Shape beanbags can be used, with children throwing them through different-shaped holes on a board. Colored beanbags might be thrown into different-colored baskets. Children can use recording sheets to keep track of the number of accurate tosses, or points can be assigned.

Figure 31

96

- Hula hoops: Provide hula hoops for children to use. Post charts showing use of the hoop on different parts of the body—waist, leg, and arm.
- Suspended yarn ball: Suspend yarn balls from the ceiling at an appropriate height for the children to practice hitting the balls. Racquets can be added.
- Aerobics area: Put out a tape of exercise records, and post pictures of persons exercising. Provide a mat, leotards, and sweatbands for children to use while exercising. Children can use recording sheets to mark the number of sit-ups, jumping jacks, and push-ups they did.
- Gymnastics: Set up a tumbling mat, balance beam, and mini-trampoline for children to use to practice gymnastic skills.
- Jump ropes: Place jump ropes in the center for children to practice using.
- Bowling: Set up bowling pins and provide a ball for children to bowl. Empty plastic soft drink bottles can be used for the bowling pins.
- Movement dice: Make large dice by covering square boxes. On one die, place the numerals 1–6. On the other die, use symbols representing different movements, such as sit-ups, jumping jacks, hops, push-ups, knee bends, and arm circles. Children roll the dice and perform the movement the specified number of times.
- Hopscotch: Use tape to mark the hopscotch board on the floor. Provide beanbags for children to toss into the squares as they play.

The preprimary centers described here provide opportunities to develop a variety of skills through interesting, developmentally appropriate activities. Teachers can choose those activities that fit the needs and interests of their students. The activities described can be modified to be used on a simplified level or a more complex level. These activities are meant to be used only as a beginning. Teachers will develop many new ideas of their own, and many excellent resource books are available. Some of these resources are listed here.

RESOURCE BOOKS

Art/Construction

Bos, Bev. *Don't Move the Muffin Tins: A Hands-Off Guide to Art for the Young Child.* Roseville, Calif.: Turn-the-Page Press, 1982.

Cherry, Clare. *Creative Art for the Developing Child: Teachers Handbook for Early Childhood Education.* 2d ed. Carthage, Ill.: Fearon Teacher Aids, 1990.

Kohl, MaryAnn F. *Scribble Cookies and Other Independent Creative Art Experiences for Children.* Bellingham, Wash.: Bright Ring Publishing, 1985.

_____. *Mudworks: Creative Clay, Dough, and Modeling Experiences.* Bellingham, Wash.: Bright Ring Publishing, 1989.

Stangl, Jean. *Magic Mixtures: Creative Fun for Little Ones Preschool– Grade 3.* Belmont, Calif.: David S. Lake Publishers, 1986.

Thompson, David. *Easy Woodstuff for Kids.* Mount Rainier, Md.: Gryphon House, 1981.

Library Communication

Catron, Carol Elaine, and Barbara Catron Parks. *Cooking Up a Story.* Minneapolis: T.S. Denison & Co., 1986.

Evans, Joy, and Jo Ellen Moore. *How to Make Books with Children.* Monterey, Calif.: Evan-Moor, 1985.

McCue, Lois. *Learning Letters Through All Five Senses: A Language Development Activity Book.* Mount Rainier, Md.: Gryphon House, 1983.

Raines, Shirley C., and Robert J. Canady. *Story S-T-R-E-T-C-H-E-R-S: Activities to Expand Children's Favorite Books.* Mount Rainier, Md.: Gryphon House, 1989.

Roundtree, Barbara S., Jean F. Gordon, Melissa B. Shuptrine, and Nancy Y. Taylor. *Creative Teaching with Puppets: Resources for Six Integrated Units.* University, Ala.: The Learning Line, 1981.

Table Games/Mathematics

Baratta-Lorton, Mary. *Workjobs: Activity Centered Learning for Early Childhood Education.* Menlo Park, Calif.: Addison-Wesley, 1972.

____. *Workjobs II: Number Activites for Early Childhood.* Menlo Park, Calif.: Addison-Wesley, 1979.

Brown, Sam Ed. *One, Two, Buckle My Shoe.* Mount Rainier, Md.: Gryphon House, 1982.

Church, Ellen Booth. *Learning Things: Games That Make Learning Fun for Children 3–8 Years Old.* Belmont, Calif.: David S. Lake Publishers, 1982.

Commins, Elaine. *Folder Game Festival for Preschool and Kindergarten.* Atlanta: Humanics Learning, 1988.

Gilbert, La Britta. *I Can Do It! I Can Do It! 135 Successful Independent Learning Activites.* Mount Rainier, Md.: Gryphon House, 1984.

Discovery

Althouse, Rosemary. *Investigating Science with Young Children.* New York: Teachers College Press, 1988.

Brown, Sam Ed. *Bubbles, Rainbows and Worms: Science Experiments for Pre-School Children.* Mount Rainier, Md.: Gryphon House, 1981.

James, Jeanne C., and Randy Granovetter. *Waterworks: Water Play Activities for Children Aged 1–6.* Lewisville, N.C.: Kaplan Press, 1987.

Johnson, Barbara. *Cup Cooking: Individual Child-Portion Picture Recipes.* Lake Alfred, Fla.: Early Educators Press, 1978.

Jurek, Dianne, and Sharon McDonald. *Discovering the World: Biological Science.* Allen, Tex.: DLM Teaching Resources, 1989.

_____. *Discovering the World: Physical Science.* Allen, Tex.: DLM Teaching Resources, 1989.

Williams, Robert A., Robert E. Rockwell, and Elizabeth A. Sherwood. *Mudpies to Magnets: A Preschool Science Curriculum.* Mount Rainier, Md.: Gryphon House, 1987.

Dramatic Play/Blocks

Fiarotta, Phyllis, and Noel Fiarotta. *Be What You Want to Be! The Complete Dress-Up and Pretend Craft Book.* New York: Workman Publishing Co., 1977.

Hirsch, Elisabeth S., ed. *The Block Book.* Washington, D.C.: National Association for the Education of Young Children, 1974.

Music/Gross Motor

Athey, Margaret, and Gwen Hotchkiss. *Complete Handbook of Music Games and Activities for Early Childhood.* West Nyack, N.Y.: Parker Publishing Co., 1982.

Brehm, Madeleine, and Nancy T. Tindell. *Movement with a Purpose: Perceptual Motor-Lesson Plans for Young Children.* West Nyack, N.Y.: Parker Publishing Co. 1983.

Burton, Leon, and William Hughes. *Music Play. Learning Activities for Young Children.* Menlo Park, Calif.: Addison-Wesley, 1979.

General

Ard, Linda, and Mabel Pitts, eds. *Room to Grow: How to Create Quality Early Childhood Environments.* Austin: Texas Association for the Education of Young Children, in press.

Beckman, Carol, Roberta Simmons, and Nancy Thomas. *Channels to Children: Early Childhood Activity Guide for Holidays and Seasons.* Colorado Springs, Colo.: Channels to Children, 1982.

Church, Ellen Booth. *Learning Things: Games That Make Learning Fun for Children 3-8 Years Old.* Belmont, Calif.: Fearon Teacher Aids, 1982.

Croft, Doreen. *An Activities Handbook for Teachers of Young Children.* 5th ed. Boston: Houghton Mifflin, 1990.

Day, Barbara. *Early Childhood Education: Creative Learning Activities.* 3d ed. New York: Macmillan, 1988.

Gottshall, Dottie, comp. "Preprimary Learning Center Activities." Nacogdoches, Tex.: Stephen F. Austin State University Printing, n.d.

Hamilton, Darlene Softley, and Bonnie Mack Fleming. *Resources for Creative Teaching in Early Childhood Education.* 2d ed. San Diego: Harcourt Brace Jovanovich, 1990.

Hibner, Dixie, and Liz Cromwell, eds. *Explore and Create.* Livonia, Mich.: Partner Press, 1979.

Indenbaum, Valerie, and Marcia Shapiro. *The Everthing Book for Teachers of Young Children.* Livonia, Mich.: Partner Press, 1983.

Schiller, Pam, and J. Rossano. *The Instant Curriculum.* Mount Rainier, Md.: Gryphon House, 1990.

Chapter 5

PRIMARY LEARNING CENTERS

The primary learning centers, which will be discussed in this chapter, are an outgrowth and expansion of the preprimary learning centers discussed in the previous chapter. Attention will be given to the rationale, organization, and appropriate actvities for each center.

The language arts centers—creative writing, reading, spelling, handwriting, and library—will be discussed first. Social studies, science, and mathematics will follow, and blocks and dramatic play are next. The last part of the chapter discusses the fine arts centers, art and music.

CREATIVE WRITING CENTER

Rationale

The creative writing center is one of the busiest in the classroom. Each day children do three things: (1) develop key words, (2) write in their personal journals, and (3) choose special activities that stimulate writing. When children write or dictate writing each day, written work becomes another form of expression. Daily writing in the early grades leads to well-constructed and meaningful reports, essays, and stories in the upper grades.

It is very difficult to separate creative writing from library, reading, spelling, and handwriting because these language arts areas are an integrated whole. Nevertheless, each of these areas is set up as a separate learning center, primarily to provide variety and choices to children as they select their work for the day. All

103

of these areas could be one very large center, a language arts center, as long as each of the academic areas is included.

When children begin to write, they usually progress in a sequence from scribbling, to showing an interest in words, to knowing a few consonant sounds and corresponding letters, to using words, to labeling pictures, to writing about personal experiences, and eventually to requesting help with the spelling of words. When a child reaches the point of asking for the spelling of words, the teacher should ask the child to think about how the word is spelled. "How do you think you spell it?" If the child can say the first letter, the word can be written like b_____ (bat). If she knows the last sound/letter, the word could be spelled b_____ t (17). This partial spelling should be encouraged in the child's writing so that thoughts can be written without frequent interruptions for "correct spelling." Even "wrong" spellings should be accepted. After more exposure to reading and writing, children will eventually correct spelling errors.

Another source that children use for spelling and writing is their "key-word ring" (17). This is a collection of personally selected words on small cards that children can read by sight. Some children begin their word ring in prekindergarten. However, most children begin key words in kindergarten. A few children, and often children new to our school, begin their ring of words in the primary or first grade classroom. All children add words to their ring during the first grade year.

Key Words

Step One

In the beginning, each child adds one key word to his ring each day. The words are added in the following manner, which is an adaptation of the approach suggested in *Key Words to Reading* (17).

1. The child selects a word. If she cannot think of a word, the teacher talks to her about things she has been doing, pets, hobbies, etc., and asks if she would like a certain word that comes from this discussion. Words important to the child, such as family names, friends' names, pets, television programs, toys, etc., are usually selected first.

A few teachers have taken word lists from readers or Dolch sight words and placed them on a ring. Doing this violates the whole purpose of this approach to beginning reading. These words should be important and powerful words to the individual child. Each key-word ring should be a personal collection of the child's most important words. The children must select these words themselves in order to be able to remember them.

2. On a 2-inch by 7-inch card cut from tagboard, the teacher writes the word as the child watches (Figure 32). During this step, the teacher talks about sound-symbol relationships. "Do you know any other words that begin like this word?" "What sound do you hear at the end of this word?" While key words is a "sight" approach initially, discussions such as the above lead the child into sound-symbol relationships.

Figure 32

3. The child traces the word with her finger. The teacher checks to see if the letters are formed correctly and corrects any incorrect formations.

4. The teacher writes another copy of the word for the child to take home. It is important for the teacher to write both of the words (for the school ring and for home) even if the child wants to write them. This way the child has a very legible copy for reference. The child can and should be encouraged to write the word at other times, in sentences or in stories.

5. The child and teacher decide on three things to do with the word. She can read it three times to a friend, write it three times on the chalkboard, or go to the spelling center and choose an activity to do with the word. This repetition helps the child place the word in her memory. Some children need more repetitions and some need less, but three repetitions seems to work for most children.

6. The child reads the other words on the ring. If she cannot remember a word, a paper clip can be placed on the word to remind the teacher to review that word. The clip can be taken off the next day if the child knows the word. If the child does not know the word, the teacher can say, "This word must not be very important to you. Let's take it off the ring. These (pointing to the other words on the ring) are the words that are important to you and those that you can read."

7. Each day the teacher asks the child to read the key word added the previous day and the other key words on the ring. Eventually, the word ring is so large that only a few words are selected for review. Paper clips help to identify the words that are more recent additions.

Since these key-word cards will be handled many times, regular paper is not sturdy enough. Many of these word strips must be made. We have a local printing shop cut as many as 6,000 at a time for us to use. This amount will usually last for a year for one classroom. This sounds like a major expense, but remember that these cards are practically the only materials used for beginning reading. No workbooks are needed. Also, these words are used for writing, spelling, and reading.

When a large set of words is accumulated, the second step is begun.

Step Two

In step two, sentences are developed. Since most of the child's words will be nouns, the teacher gives the child a verb such as "loves," which will connect several of the child's words on his ring. Then the child can write sentences, such as "Paige loves Heidi" or "Mommy loves Paige." Several other words can be used very successfully at this point, including *likes, sees, has,* and *hugs.* These connecting words allow children to use many key words in various arrangements to create sentences. The child first arranges the key-word cards. Then he writes the sentences.

Step Three

Step three involves the writing of sentences or stories by the child. During this step, writing becomes very important to the child. First, two sentences are written. Eventually, stories are written. These sentences and short stories can be illustrated and shared with the class members.

Step Four

Step four of this process moves the child into primers or easy books that have many of the words that are already on the child's key-word ring.

Assessment of Reading

As the teacher works with individual children in the creative writing center, she records information in the child's reading folder, which is kept in a bin in this center. This folder contains a checklist of reading skills (see Reading Center below). The folder also contains a list of books read by the child and a dated record of individual key words or reading sessions with the teacher, such as the one below:

Date	Notes
11-16-9X	Added "basketball" to key words. Tom knew the sound of "b" and that basketball was two words. Discussed compound words.
11-18-9X	Tom read all of his key words. Added "ballgame." Play compound word dominoes next time.

Journal Writing

Each child writes in a journal daily. Key words can be written and illustrated early. Sentences can be dictated by the child and written by the teacher or a parent volunteer. Eventually, each child writes sentences and stories. The teacher should read each journal weekly, writing comments such as these:

	Journal Entry	Teacher's Comments
3/4/9X	Yesterday I went to granddad's house.	That must have been fun.
	We went fishing.	
	I have a new puppy.	I'd like to see him.
	His name is "Old Yeller."	Wow!
	I rided my bike to Paige's house.	You must have been tired.

He should never make corrections. But, in the reading folder or on a small card, he can note anything he needs to work on with the child individually or during small-group time.

The journal is a common spiral-bound notebook. The child keeps a piece of carbon paper in it and makes a copy of each story to take home. One copy stays in the classroom. These journals are excellent records of progress as they show the emerging literacy of the child.

In addition to key words and the journal (which are daily assignments), other activities are placed in the creative writing center to stimulate writing. Petreshene (13) has many excellent ideas for story starters.

Organization

This center should have shelf space for activities, a large pegboard for displaying key words, and a large square table where children can work. Journals can be housed in a bin on top of the shelves. Picture dictionaries and a variety of writing materials should always be available. An example of a creative writing center is sketched in Figure 33.

Activities

- Feely box: Each day place an object (rock, rubber band, small toy, etc.) in the box. The children write about what they think is in the box.

- Make a pennant: Have children think of a new football team and write the team name on the pennant.

- Monday story: Make copies of the following for students to fill in:

  This weekend I went to _____ with my _____ . We saw a _____ . "I want to buy the _____ ," I said. We decided to _____ . Tomorrow I want to _____ .
  The End.

- Draw a picture: The children write a word or sentence about the picture.

- If I were a. . . .: Have children choose a picture card of

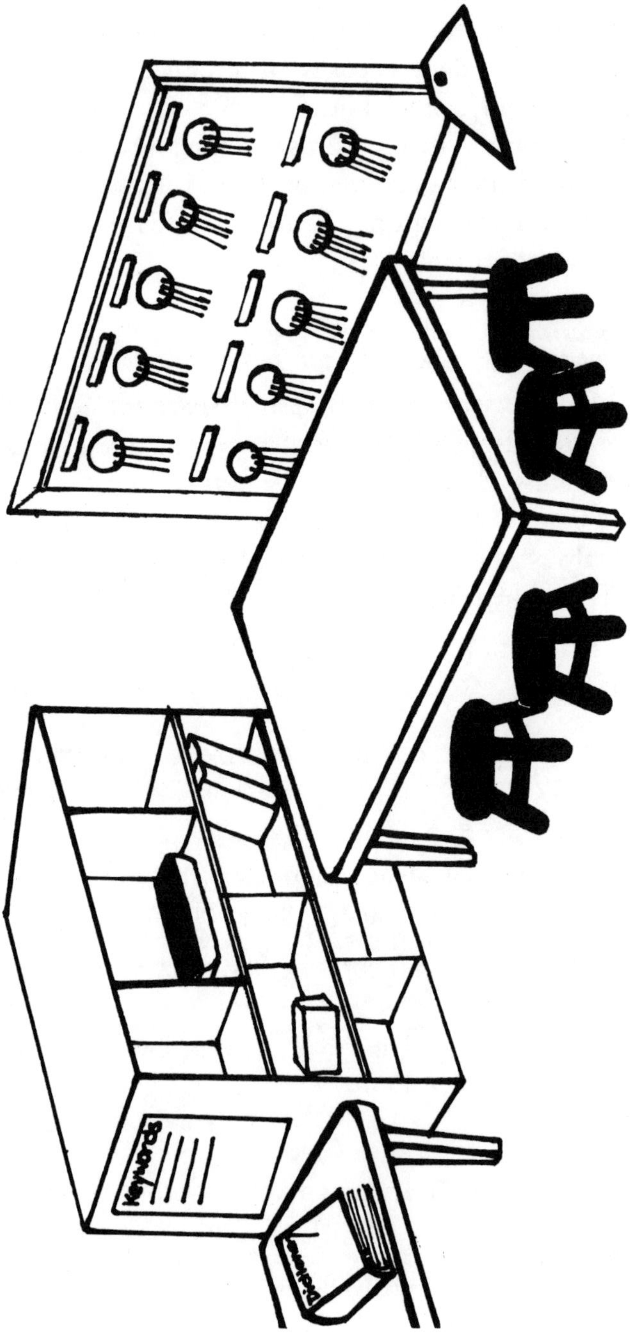

Figure 33

110

a dog, a car, a vacuum cleaner, etc., and write what they would do.

- Kite tales: Children each choose three key words and write them in the kite tails.
- The blob: Have children choose a blob and draw a picture or write a sentence about their blob.
- Story words: Children take words out of a familiar story and write a sentence with those words.
- Art blottos: In the art center, children fold paper in half. They place one scoop of paint in the center, press the paper together, and let it dry. In creative writing, they write a sentence about what they made. "This is a _____ ."
- The balloon story: Children complete this story: "One day, when I was very small, I jumped into a balloon and floated away. . . ."
- I can story: Children fill in the blanks.
  "I can _____ .
  I can _____ .
  I can _____ .
  But the best thing I can do is _____ ."
- Telephone's ringing: Children complete the sentences. "Hello, this is _____ . Would you like to _____ ?"
- Publishing: Children write and publish a monthly magazine of stories and poems.
- Letter writing: Have the children write a letter to say thank you, initiate an excursion, etc.
- Imaginary stories: Children complete this story: "One day I was walking in the woods and heard a noise. . . ."
- Story writing: Children follow up by writing a story such as "The Three Wishes": "If I had a wish, I would want. . . ."
- Interview: Children interview the teacher about a topic. The teacher says, "Last year I went to New York." The child asks, "How did you go?"
- News events: Children write about a tornado, the fair or circus, a new president, etc.

111

- Fill-in stories: Children write stories about the following:

"Happiness is. . . ."
"How I feel about. . . ."
"What if. . . ."
"Red is. . . ."
"A friend is. . . ."
"I don't like people who. . . ."
"I like people. . . ."
"When it's raining. . . ."
"If I had a magic wand. . . ."
"The best thing about me is. . . ."

READING CENTER

Rationale

In a learning center classroom, reading is integrated in many different ways. It is taught during total-group times, small-group times, individual reading conferences, sharing times, and transitional activities and in many different learning centers. Creative writing, spelling, and reading specifically stress reading.

All the other learning centers encourage children to use reading in a functional manner to read self-directional symbol charts, such as the one shown in Figure 34. To participate in the activities in the centers, children eagerly read these charts. Symbol charts begin with picture reading for four- and five-year-olds and move to reading pictures and words in the primary grades. By second and third grade, many children can read directions found on task cards, such as the one in Figure 35. By using symbol charts and task cards, reading becomes a key to opening new games and experiences in the learning centers.

Organization

The reading center is organized with shelf space for 15 to 18 games or activities. Four to six children usually use tables in

Figure 34

Figure 35

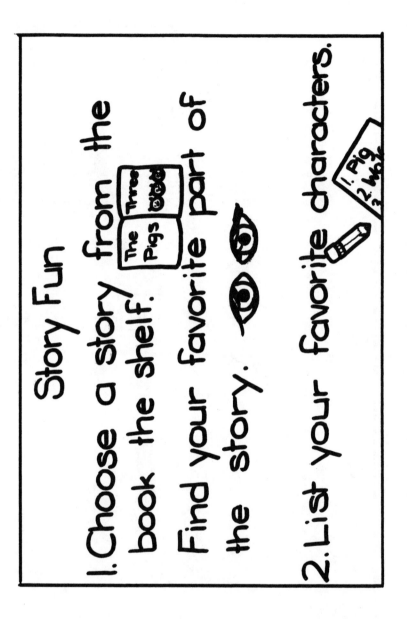

Story Fun

1. Choose a story from the book the shelf.

Find your favorite part of the story.

2. List your favorite characters.

this center at the same time. Placing the reading and creative writing centers next to each other allows access by the teacher to reading assessment folders as she works in either center. The reading assessment folder contains two things, a checklist of reading skills and a record of individual conferences (11). Examples of these forms are shown in Figures 36 and 37.

Each reading game or activity is placed on a separate section of the reading shelf. On the shelf beside most games or activities are lists containing the names of the children who are to complete the activity (Figure 38). Games are selected specifically for certain children. Other children besides those listed may play the games after they complete the games that are assigned to them. We make many blank cards, laminate them, and then write the children's names on them with transparency markers or permanent felt pens. These cards are used over and over. Transparency markers can be erased with water. Hair spray can be used to erase permanent markers.

Most reading games can be designed around certain game strategies. These game strategies can be varied to make many games for reading—for example, Bingo, Lotto, trail games, Old Maid, Go Fish, puzzles, Concentration or Memory, sorting, matching, and tachistoscope are just a few.

Since there are so many sources for reading games, only a few games will be described here. For a more complete listing, refer to the sources listed at the end of the chapter.

Activities

Reading Games for the First Level

Key-Word Activities. Since our children begin to read using the key-word approach described in relation to the creative writing center, several key-word activities are offered in the reading center each week.

Figure 36

```
┌─────────────────────────────────────────────────────────────┐
│                    READING CHECKLIST                          │
│                                                               │
│  Reading initial, medial, final consonants                    │
│                                                               │
│  A.      b      _____   _____   _____          │
│          c      _____   _____   _____          │
│          d      _____   _____   _____          │
│          f      _____   _____   _____          │
│          g      _____   _____   _____          │
│          h      _____   _____   _____          │
│          j      _____   _____   _____          │
│          k      _____   _____   _____          │
│          l      _____   _____   _____          │
│          m      _____   _____   _____          │
│          n      _____   _____   _____          │
│          p      _____   _____   _____          │
│          q      _____   _____   _____          │
│          r      _____   _____   _____          │
│          s      _____   _____   _____          │
│          t      _____   _____   _____          │
│          v      _____   _____   _____          │
│          w      _____   _____   _____          │
│          x      _____   _____   _____          │
│          y      _____   _____   _____          │
│          z      _____   _____   _____          │
│                                                               │
│  Vowels                                                       │
│                 Short        Long                             │
│          a      _____   _____                       │
│          e      _____   _____                       │
│          i      _____   _____                       │
│          o      _____   _____                       │
│          u      _____   _____                       │
│                                                               │
│  Structural Analysis                                          │
│          ed     _____                                    │
│          compound words (cowboy, into)  _____            │
│                                                               │
│  B.  Basic Sight Words                                        │
│                                                               │
│                                                               │
│  C.  Comprehension                                            │
│          main idea  _____                                │
│          recall facts and details  _____                 │
│                                                               │
│                                                               │
│                                                               │
└─────────────────────────────────────────────────────────────┘
```

Figure 37

Date	Child's Reading Conference Form	
	Remarks/Assignments	Signatures

Figure 38

Near the reading and creative writing centers at our school is a small table where the teacher writes key words for children each day. A chart, such as the one in Figure 39, is displayed where children write the key word they have selected for the day. By glancing at the chart, the teacher can tell who has and has not written a key word for the day.

Figure 39

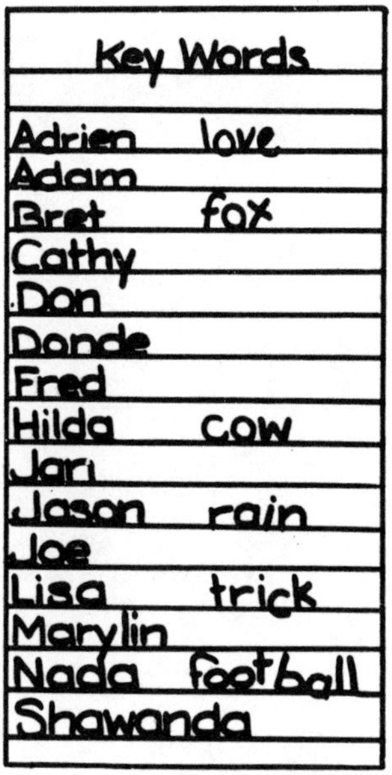

Key Words	
Adrien	love
Adam	
Bret	fox
Cathy	
Don	
Donde	
Fred	
Hilda	cow
Jari	
Jason	rain
Joe	
Lisa	trick
Marylin	
Nada	football
Shawanda	

Here are some ways children can practice their key word.

Write it on the chalkboard (use colored chalk).

Write it on a Magic Slate.

If the child has dictated a story, write it on the back of the story three times.

Write it with letter stamps.

Write it in cornmeal, salt, or flour.

Trace it with three crayons (rainbow word).

Trace it on felt or sandpaper with pencil finger.

Trace it on a carpet square with pencil finger.

Place the word under a wire screen board and trace it.

Trace it on a friend's or teacher's back.

Type it.

Form it with clay.

Use letter stencils to write it.

Use magnetic letters to write it.

Use sealed plastic bags with mustard, ketchup, or jello inside. Write word with pencil finger.

Use white chalk on dark paper.

Games Developing Letter Recognition

- Old Maid: Children play Old Maid with letter cards (Figure 40). Books of two letters make a pair. The old maid can be a sticker of any kind. Use large butter tub lids with a brad in the middle as a holder for the cards.

Figure 40

- Go Fish: Children play Go Fish using the same cards as for Old Maid. Each child has seven cards. Children take turns calling for each letter. If no one has the letter, the child draws or fishes from the deck.
- Letter Lotto: Make two poster board Lotto boards 12 inches by 12 inches in size. They should be marked off into 12 squares, with a letter on each square. Place different letters on each board. Make small cards for each letter. Children draw cards and match them to the letters on the board. The first child to cover his board is the winner.
- Letter Bingo: Make this game like Lotto, except have the letters on each board in a different order.
- Letter Concentration: Make two sets of 26 cards, with 2 cards for each letter. All cards are placed face down. The child turns over two cards. If they match, she keeps them. If they do not, she turns them back over. Then the next child tries to make a match. The winner is the child with the most matches (Figure 41).

Figure 41

Games Developing Initial Consonant Sounds

- Sounds trail game: Choose four consonants. Make a trail game with these letters on each square. Make cards with pictures beginning with these sounds. Each child draws a card. If he can say the letter the picture begins with, he moves his marker to that space (Figure 42).

Figure 42

- Sorting sounds: Have children sort objects such as pencils, scissors, and small toys into large cans or boxes by beginning sounds. Erasers and children's party favors make good objects to sort (Figure 43).

Figure 43

- Feely box: Place various objects in a bag or feely box. Children take turns reaching into and matching objects to a board with letters written on it. The first to complete the board wins (Figure 44).

Figure 44

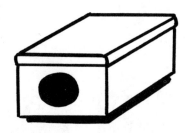

- Sound go fishing: Make 39 playing cards with 13 sounds, each represented by 3 cards. (A cat, a cookie, and a car could represent "C.") Each player gets six cards. The remaining cards are the deck from which children fish. The first player calls for all of the cards beginning with C. If no one has any, she "goes fishing" from the deck. Children collect books of three.

Games Developing Short Vowels

Suggested pictures for short vowels are listed below:

- *a* — pad, tag, jam, ham, cat, man, pan
  e — egg, well, pet, red, hen, ten
  i — ship, Indian, pin, pig, six, lid
  o — dog, doll, box, fox, toys, log
  u — umbrella, sun, duck, hut, tub, cub, nut

- Short-vowel Lotto: Prepare two boards with the vowel sounds *a*, *o*, and *u*. (*e*, *i*, and *y* can be added later.) Prepare 12 pictures for each sound. (Readiness workbooks and stickers are good sources for pictures.) Children take turns drawing cards with pictures of the sound. The first to fill the board wins (Figure 45).

Figure 45

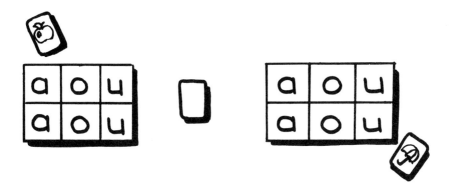

- Vowel fishing: Use cards from short-vowel Lotto and play Go Fish (or Old Maid).
- Vowel Concentration: Make pairs of pictures. As children turn over pairs, they say the short vowel in the pair.
- Short vowel dominoes: Place pictures of short-vowel words on dominoes. Children play by matching vowel sounds in words. The first one to use all dominoes wins (Figure 46).

Figure 46

Reading Games for Upper Levels

Have children do the following:
- State an opinion that you have about a subject. Read some books and/or consult reference books for information. Share the opinions of authorities with the class.
- Make a book of famous people. Include place of birth, special characteristics and acts for which the person is

famous, hobbies, and anything of special interest. (This could be a class project or an individual project.)

- Read about people in another country, and write a short report on the topic "What surprised me most when I read about _____ ."
- Read several books about different countries. As you read them, pretend that you are traveling in that country. Keep a travel diary telling of your experience in that country as you read about it.
- Have a small group plan a panel discussion in which they discuss the lives of famous artists about whom they have read. The discussion could include
  1. A contrast of the childhood of people
  2. What may have happened to influence their later life
  3. What they did to make them famous
  4. What struggles they faced to accomplish their goals.

- Read about the life of a famous composer. Bring to class a recording of one of his or her famous compositions. Play the record and explain it.
- Select some of the events that took place in a book. Using these events, make up a newspaper that could have been printed in the town where the story book took place. The headlines would be something very important that took place. The news stories would contain interesting events of the story.
- Prepare a collection of something you have read about (rocks, erasers, stamps, etc.), with appropriate information for an exhibit.
- Plan a pantomime and have other children guess the title of the books.
- As a class project, prepare a book fair to share books with other classes.
- Write an additional stanza to a poem you have read.

SPELLING CENTER

Rationale/Organization

Spelling is one of the easiest subjects to individualize and organize into a learning center format. Basically, the teacher should do two things: (1) select the words to be learned, and (2) construct a set of materials.

The child has four tasks each week: (1) he selects 5 to 10 words to study for the week, (2) he practices the words in a variety of ways in the spelling center, (3) he takes a test over the spelling words each week, and (4) he makes a new list of words, adding any words missed from the previous test.

Let's look at the teacher's responsibilities in initiating this center.

Selecting the Spelling Lists

For beginning spellers, words should be grouped according to simplicity, use, and phonic and structural commonalities. Many word lists are available for use in the spelling center. Spelling textbooks provide the most commonly used lists.

Petreshene (12) gives a very useful and complete guide to individualized spelling. Petreshene (13) has also prepared a list of spelling words from three widely used lists: Madden-Carlson, Rinsland, and Dolch. This list, which has been used very successfully in our primary classroom, is included in the supplement to her book.

Petreshene uses seven lists of spelling words for her program. These lists include short-vowel words; short-vowel and long-vowel words, blends, and digraphs; a basic spelling vocabulary; 100 words most often misspelled by children in the elementary grades; spelling demons; 200 important spelling words for upper grade students; and words with specific phonetic elements. A less-structured approach would consist of a list of words from a spelling text. Children would choose 10 words to study each week. Other words that can be studied include key words, holiday words, and words from units of study in science or social studies.

The Spelling Materials

Next, the teacher should create the spelling materials for each child to use. Two sets of materials need to be available in the spelling center each week. Once they are constructed, they are used over and over again.

These materials are "School Words/Home Words" and "My Spelling Test." "School Words/Home Words" (Figure 47) is designed so that the child can copy the 10 words to be studied each week onto this sheet. Then the child makes a second copy on the right side of the paper for a take-home copy. The paper is cut into two pieces—one for home and one for school.

"My Spelling Test" (Figure 48) should be reproduced on colored paper. Each week the child takes a spelling test on this sheet. The sheets can be saved and stapled together to make a booklet for each child.

Both "School Words/Home Words" and "My Spelling Test" are kept in stacks on the spelling center shelves.

Each day the child goes to the spelling center. On Monday the child selects 5 to 10 words to study during the week and makes two lists of these words on the form called "School Words/Home Words." In addition, some teachers encourage children to choose at least one special word from their key-word ring. One copy of the words stays in the center, and one copy may be taken home.

Then the child chooses a way to study the words from the activities provided in the center. Usually three activities are available for practice. Each day the child studies the words in at least one way.

On Friday, the child takes a test over the words she selected and studied during the week. The test can be given to seven or eight children at a time by stacking their "School Words" in the order of the children and giving each child a word from her list.

Not all children are "Spelling Friends" at the beginning of the year. Our teachers made this a special center that is added when children can read a large group of key words. Therefore, it becomes a source of pride for the children when they become "Spelling Friends."

Figure 47

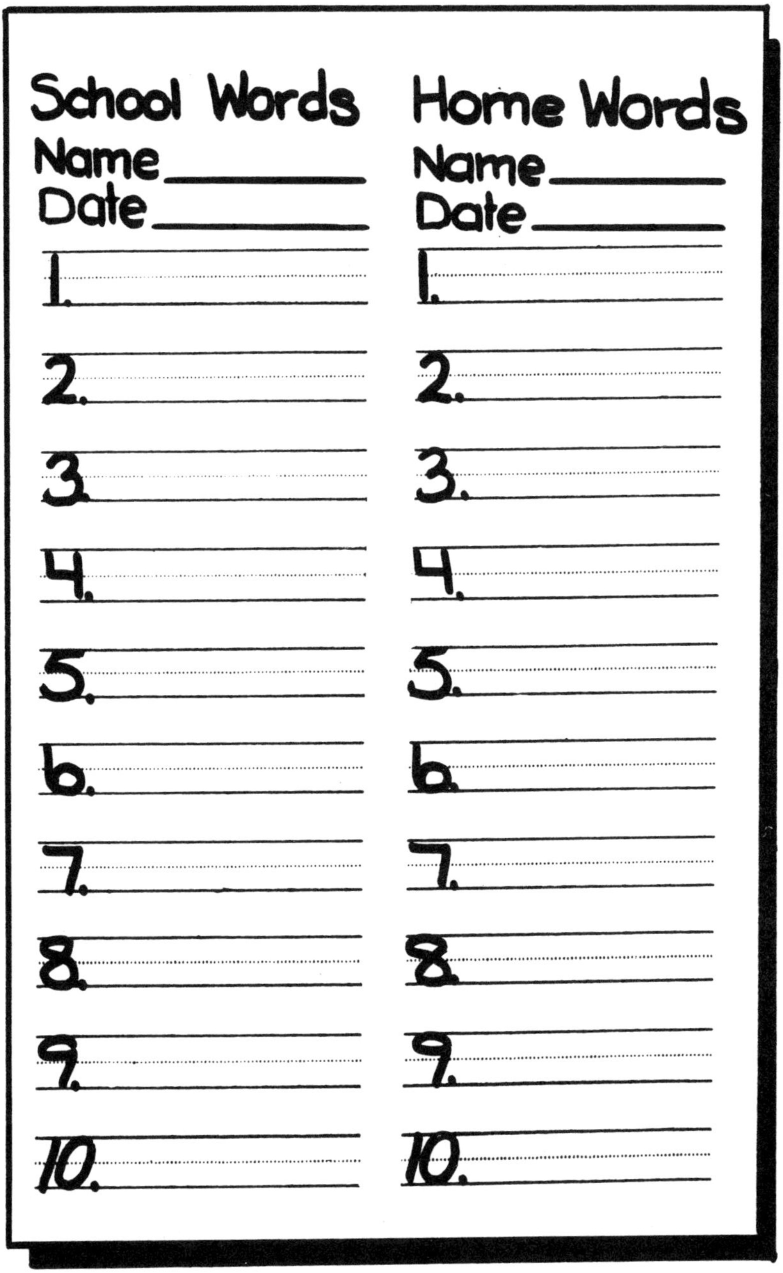

School Words	Home Words
Name_____	Name_____
Date_____	Date_____
1.	1.
2.	2.
3.	3.
4.	4.
5.	5.
6.	6.
7.	7.
8.	8.
9.	9.
10.	10.

Figure 48

My Spelling Test

Name _____

Date _____

1.

2.

3.

4.

5.

6.

7.

8.

9.

10.

In the beginning, as few as three words can be studied each week. Some teachers begin with only 3 and move to 5 and then 10 words.

Another way to begin spelling is to study initial and ending consonants. Children can practice certain consonant sounds and then take a spelling test over words, writing only the beginning and ending sound (h __ t for hat). Later short vowels could be added.

Activities

Have children select activities from the following list to practice their spelling words:

- Spell words with letters written on plastic milk carton lids (Figure 49).

Figure 49

- Make clay or play dough words (Figure 50).

Figure 50

- Write words on a Magic Slate (Figure 51).

Figure 51

- Spell words with dice with a letter on each side (Figure 52).

Figure 52

- Scramble each spelling word. Then spell it (Figure 53).

Figure 53

- Spell words on a magnetic board (Figure 54).

Figure 54

- Color a small card, cover it with black crayon, and scratch the word out (Figure 55).

Figure 55

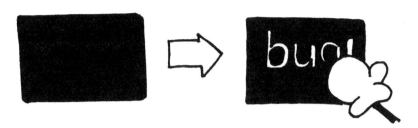

- Stamp letters of words with commercial letters and a stamp pad (Figure 56).

Figure 56

- Spell words with cereal loops. Then eat them (Figure 57).

Figure 57

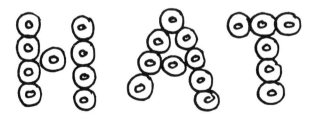

- Make a word cloud (Figure 58).

Figure 58

- Write the words with stikki-wikki (Figure 59).

Figure 59

- Invisible words: Write the words on dark-colored construction paper with bleach and cotton swabs (Figure 60).

Figure 60

- Make words of yarn; glue on small cards (Figure 61).

Figure 61

- Alphabetize words (Figure 62).

Figure 62

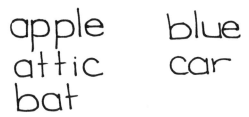

- Write the words on the flannelboard (Figure 63).

Figure 63

- Draw pictures of each word. Write the word on the picture (Figure 64).

Figure 64

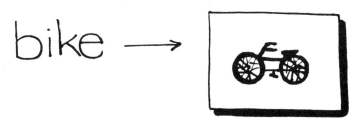

- Write words in a pan of salt (Figure 65).

Figure 65

- Write the words on the chalkboard (Figure 66).

Figure 66

- Write the words using carbon paper and two sheets of typing paper (Figure 67).

Figure 67

- Write words with a felt pen on balloons. Blow up the balloons (Figure 68).

Figure 68

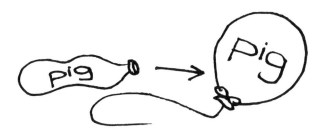

- Make pipe cleaner words (Figure 69).

Figure 69

- Write the words out of cereal letters. Then eat them (Figure 70).

Figure 70

HANDWRITING CENTER

Rationale/Organization

The handwriting center is an area where children practice individual letter formations and write sentences and short narratives. Before children are dismissed into learning centers and when they are still in a group activity (usually early in the morning), the teacher writes a letter on the chalkboard. He talks about how the letter is formed. Sometimes the teacher writes it incorrectly and asks the class to tell him what is wrong with it. The teacher might write several examples of the letter and ask them to select the one that is best and to tell why. In this way the letter formation is previewed.

Next the teacher previews what the children should do when they go to the handwriting center that day. Each child has a folder in this center with her name on it. The teacher places five letter pages (Figure 71) in the folder for the week. These letter pages are half sheets of ruled paper with dotted half-lines that have individual letters on each page. A full sheet of paper would be too tiring to complete at one time.

The child completes the page or letter sheet that was previewed during the morning group time and places it back in her folder. At the end of the week, the teacher checks the folder, commenting about or circling properly formed letters. He staples these pages in the handwriting folder for future reference and parent conferences. He also notes letters that need more practice on the inside of the folder. Later, after all the letters have been introduced, he can place only the letter sheets that need to be reviewed in the folder.

At the beginning of second grade, the teacher can give a diagnostic handwriting test by having the children write each letter in their best writing. He can circle the letters that need practicing and then place practice sheets in the handwriting folder.

In the third grade, cursive letters are usually introduced one per day at group time and then practiced in the handwriting center.

The following sequence for introducing the manuscript letters works well:

l, i, t, a, c, d, o

q, g, j, p, b, k

n, m, h, r, v, y, w, x, z

f, s, u, e

This group of letters begins with the line letters, then goes to the "c" letters, curved letters, hump letters, and slant letters, and then to the "leftover" letters. The cursive letters are grouped in a different manner with easier letters first (Figure 72). Then they build on strokes developed previously. In addition to the half sheets of paper with individual letters, other copy work can be made by reproducing poems, jokes, address books, class telephone books, and jump-rope jingles. As children copy, they practice their handwriting. Our children work in this center each day for a short period. The teacher changes activities weekly, leaving some activities for longer periods of time depending on interest.

Some excellent sources for copy-work materials are listed at the end of this chapter. Figure 73 shows a sketch of a handwriting center.

Figure 71

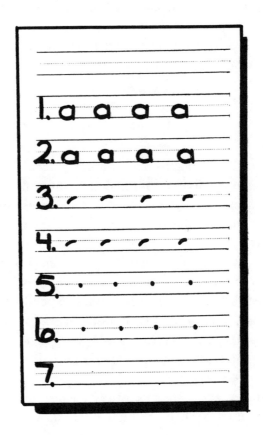

Figure 72

138

Figure 73

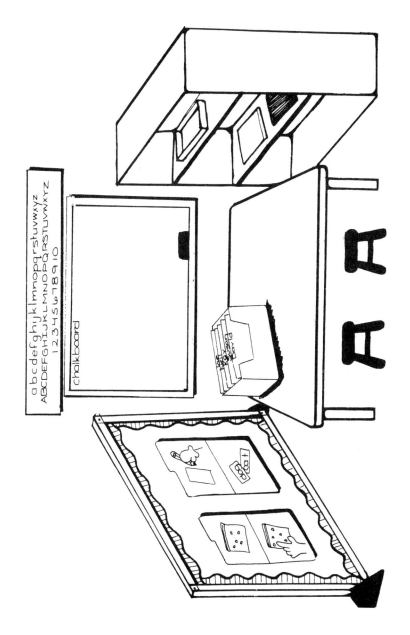

Activities

- Autograph book: Provide small books covered with wallpaper. Each child signs the books (Figure 74).

Figure 74

- Word trace: Children choose a key word, and trace it three times with different colors (Figure 75).

Figure 75

- Pattern continuation: Start a pattern. The children continue the pattern (Figure 76).

Figure 76

- Chalkboard painting: Children choose a key word and write it with a paintbrush and water on the chalkboard (Figure 77).

Figure 77

- Writing friends' names: Children choose a friend's name and write it (Figure 78).

Figure 78

- Telephone books: Have children copy friends' names and telephone numbers from a chart (Figure 79).

Figure 79

- Trace a word: Write words on 5 inch by 8 inch index cards with yellow markers. Draw a picture of the word or glue an object on the card. Laminate. The child traces over the word with a transparency marker. Then the cards are wiped off with a damp sponge and used again (Figure 80).

Figure 80

- ABC words: Children choose five key words and write them in ABC order with a transparency pen (Figure 81).

Figure 81

- Trace a shape: Have children choose a shape, trace the shape, and write its name (Figure 82).

Figure 82

- Cornmeal writing: Children choose a key word, write the word in cornmeal, and spell the word out loud (Figure 83).

Figure 83

- Best letter: Children choose five letters. Then they write each one three times, and circle the best letter (Figure 84).

Figure 84

- Rainbow words: Children choose a key word and write it in five colors with markers (Figure 85).

Figure 85

- Flavor words: Children choose a key word, and write it with two different scented markers.

- Theme words: Make a chart of words that highlight themes or holidays, such as Halloween, Thanksgiving, Chinese, Dinosaur, or space words. Children then choose words to write (Figure 86).

Figure 86

LIBRARY CENTER

Rationale

Free reading becomes an important part of the curriculum during the primary years, as the emphasis moves from oral to written language. As children begin to actually read, this center becomes an area in the room where they enjoy reading books over and over again, just as they enjoyed hearing stories over and over when they were younger. "Big Books" and books that have been shared at group time can be enjoyed again during center time. As children mature into more independent readers, this center becomes not only a reading area, but also a research area where projects that started in reading, science, and other areas are investigated.

Organization

The primary library center should accommodate four to five children at a time. Good children's books, as well as basal readers, reference books, dictionaries, and children's magazines, are located in this center. Some books are shelved with the spines facing outward. Others are displayed with the front showing.

In addition to books, usually three to five other manipulative activities are placed on tables or shelves in this center. These activities are varied weekly according to the interests and needs of the children.

Activities

- Read to your animal: Children choose a stuffed animal and read a book to it.
- Dial-a-friend: Children choose five friends' phone numbers from cards and dial the numbers on a play or real phone.
- Shapes and words: Children choose five shapes. Then they choose the cards that match the shapes (Figure 87).

Figure 87

145

- Word books: Provide small books. Children find words they know in magazines, cut them out, and glue them in the books.
- Tape a story: Children choose a set of picture cards. They use them to tell a story that is tape-recorded and then listen to their story.
- Children's books: Child-authored books developed in creative writing should be housed in the library center for all the children to read.
- Bookmarks: Children choose a book, read the book, and make a bookmark about the story.
- Peg letters: Write letters or character names from books on cards. Children choose a card and write the name with pegs.
- Listen and draw: Children tape a short descriptive story ("A huge creature with purple knobs on its head, seven legs, pink polka dots, and green eyes came toward me. . . ."). Then they draw a picture of the "thing" described.
- My favorite part: Children read a book. Then they write their favorite part and read it at group time. Other children guess which story it was.
- Name the character: Children take a flannelboard character, and find the character's name. Then they place these on the flannelboard.
- Books and titles: Children match the book with the title.
- Story strips: Summarize a favorite story in three to five statements written on strips. Children organize the strips in the order that they happened.
- Act out the story: Provide props for a favorite story, such as Rapunzel. Children then act it out.
- Book report: A sample form is shown in Figure 88.

Figure 88

Book Report

1. Book Title _____
2. How well did you read? ☺ 😐 ☹
3. Write 3 new words?

_____ _____ _____

4. Did you like the story? ☺ 😐 ☹
5. Draw the part you like best.

SOCIAL STUDIES CENTER

Rationale

Most primary grades have social studies textbooks. These books can serve as a guide for the organization of social studies learning center activities. Various types of activities can be found in the social studies center—slides, filmstrips, reports, games, cooking, graphing, simulation activites, role playing, and puppets. Primary social studies is usually organized around the themes of self-concept, friendship, families, neighborhoods, communities, holidays, map and globe skills, cultures, economics, and beginning history. Using state or local school objectives, activities can be developed that allow children to work independently, in small groups, and in total groups. Social studies center activites provide the best vehicle for independent and small-group activities. The primary years are a very important time for the development of the self. Samuels (15) states that there are four aspects of the self: body self, cognitive self, social self, and self-esteem. The development of body self, cognitive self, social self, and self-esteem can be enhanced through activities in this center. The primary years are also a very important time for children to develop friendships. During this time, the child is becoming much less egocentric and more interested in developing close relations with others. Learning how to enter a group, how to show friendship, what makes a good friend, and how to be a friend are important social studies concepts highlighted in this center.

Organization

The social studies center should be located near an electrical outlet for audio-visual equipment. Shelf space for four or five activities is needed. Table space for two to four children should also be provided. Certain activities require reference materials, globes, and maps.

Activities

The following are described as examples of appropriate social studies center activities. These activities highlight self-concept, friendship, and map skills.

Developing Self-Esteem

- Self-pictures: Children paint pictures of themselves on a mirror using finger paint.
- "Me" books: Children make "Me" books.

  I am _____.
  I have _____hair.
  I have _____eyes.
  _____loves me.
  _____loves me.
  My friend is _____.
  I can _____ .

- "I Feel": Children choose five words that describe them, such as *happy, kind, sad, tough, loud, strong,* and *good.* Each child draws a picture of himself being one of those words. Then he writes the word on the back of the picture and asks friends to guess which word he used to describe himself.

- "I Like": Children write "I Like" stories.

  I like to eat _____ .
  I like the color _____ .
  I like the TV show _____ .
  I like to play _____ .
  When I go outside, I like to _____ .
  One day I _____ .
  My favorite center is _____ .

- Then they exchange "I Like" stories at group time and guess whom each story describes.

- Name Concentration: Children play Concentration using cards with children's names written on them. They read the names as they turn the cards over.
- Latch board pictures: Place pictures of children behind latch board doors. Children open the doors and see pictures of themselves.
- Baby pictures match: Children match baby pictures with school pictures of each child.
- Paper plate faces: Children make paper plate faces. They attach strips of hair (construction paper) to the plates that have adjectives describing the child. (Have a chart listing appropriate adjectives for reference.)
- Feelings trail game: Make a trail game of happy, sad, angry, and surprised faces (Figure 89). The child spins a spinner, moves her marker, and tells something that makes her feel like the picture on which she landed.

Figure 89

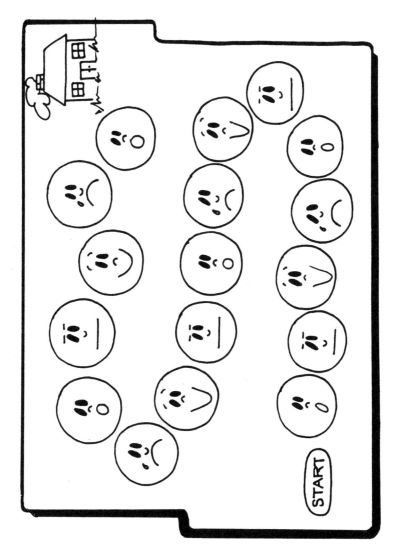

151

Being and Making Friends

- Making friends: Children choose two puppets or paper dolls who want to be friends. They then practice having the "people" meet and initiate a conversation. (Sometimes young children have difficulty introducing themselves.)
- Helping others: Find several pictures of people helping others. Children choose a picture and pantomime the action for another child to guess.
- Friends who help us feel good: Children write stories about what another child has done to make them feel good.

    _____ makes me feel good.
    He/She _____ .

- Matching feelings: Children find pictures of people showing various emotions and match these pictures with word cards listing the emotions (for example, happy, sad, angry, and surprised.)
- Sharing: Place gum, small pieces of candy, or other edible items in the center. At preview time, establish a rule: the only way to get a piece is to be given one by a friend. Later discuss what happened at group time.
- Friendship books: Place books about friends in the center for children to read. Make a chart of characters in the books. List words that describe the characters in the books.
- Problems: Record several conflict situations on a tape recorder. Ask two children to write or record a solution to each conflict. Discuss these conflicts and solutions at group time. Emphasize the feelings of each person and the consequences of each solution.

Making Maps

- Mapping the room: Mark the walls of the classroom with north (N), south (S), east (E), and west (W). Place a map of the classroom in the center. Make stars for particular places in the room. Each place should have a word from a poem placed on the wall or furniture. The child follows the map and copies the words, completing the rhyme.

- Building the school: Children use unit blocks, small houses, blue paper lakes, brown streets, trees, and other features to build the area near the school.
- My street: Ask the children to draw a map of the street where they live, showing houses and other buildings.
- Going on a trip: Two to four children can play this trail game. Each child spins a spinner showing north, east, south, west, and two free spaces. Then she spins another spinner showing the number of spaces to move. Each child has a "car" mover. She drives the car the appropriate number of spaces. The goal is to get "off" the board ending up at the park, home, school, or mall (Figure 90).

SCIENCE CENTER

Rationale

In the primary grades, the discovery center becomes the science center. While both open-ended and single-purpose activities are still available, investigations of physical matter and the recording of findings become central to the activities in this center. As children begin to read, science activities become investigations integrating reading and writing. Sharing findings with classmates gives purpose to these investigations.

Organization

In the first and second grades, four or five activities are available in the science center at a time. Each day the children investigate one of the four or five activities. One day each week children read and discuss the reading in their science books. Although shelves may be needed for some activities, most of the activities require work spaces such as small tables. Other materials that are needed are "turn-in" boxes for recording pages, worksheets, and pencils.

Figure 90

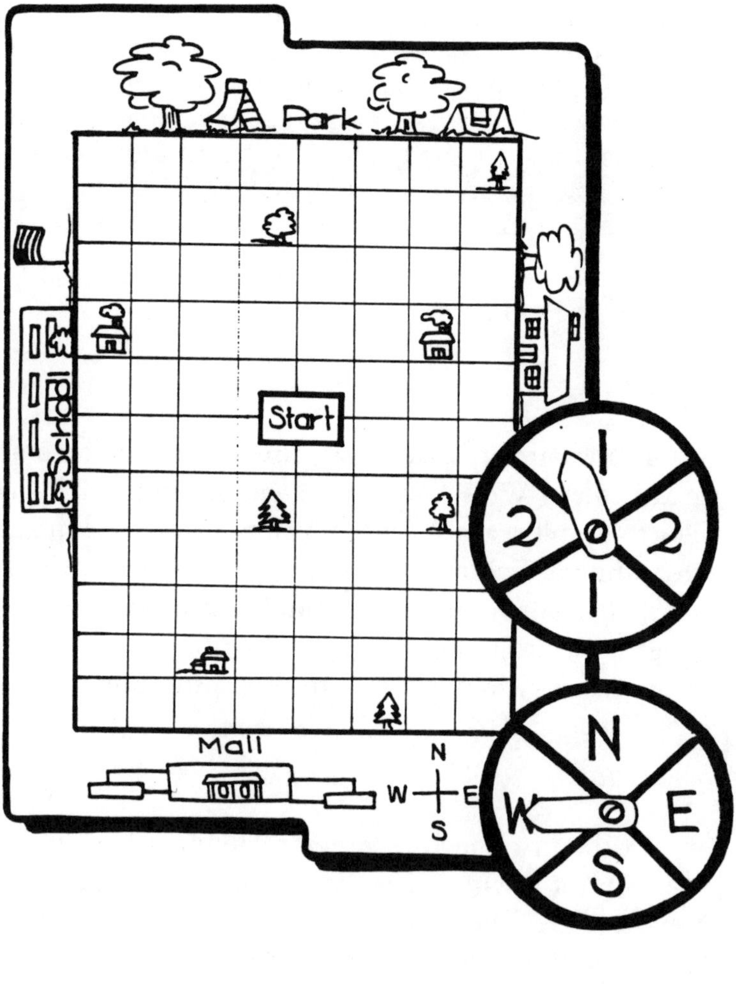

154

The activities in this center should follow themes or units, such as the senses, air, water, color, space, the earth, machines, measurements, plants, animals, motion, temperature, electricity, magnets, etc. Units are found in many science textbooks. Even though science textbooks are available, the science center activities should provides hands-on exploration of real materials. Many science textbooks have supplementary kits of materials that are excellent sources for science center activities and equipment. A sketch of a science center is shown in Figure 91 (on p. 156).

Activities

- Cracking nuts: Place the pecans or other nuts on a tray. Children try to crack them, first with their hands, and then with a nutcracker.
- Pulley board: Children nail five large spools on one board and three large spools on another board. Then they connect spools with large rubber bands and make a pennant or pinwheel turn by turning the pulley (Figure 92).

Figure 92

Figure 91

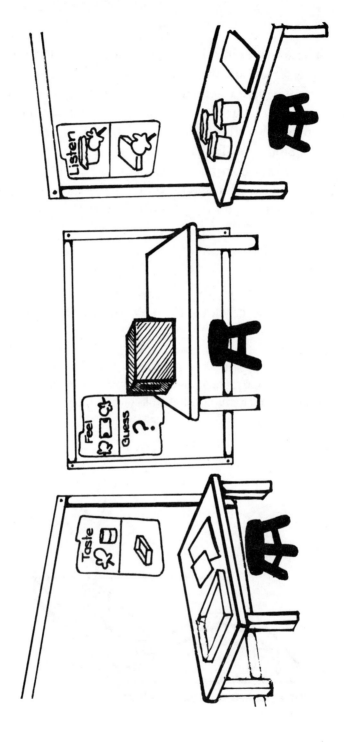

156

- Class wheel book: Children find pictures of objects with wheels in a catalog.
- Make a wagon: Children make a wagon out of a box, using straws and plastic drink lids for the axle and wheels. They attach the axle to the box with pipe cleaners.
- Gears: Place several toys and tools that have gears (egg beaters, bicycle, clock, drill) on a tray for children to manipulate. They match the tools to pictures showing their use.
- Make gears: Children place six toothpicks around the edge of a round piece of styrofoam. They place the styrofoam on a note board with a nail in the center and make a second gear that turns the first one (Figure 93).

Figure 93

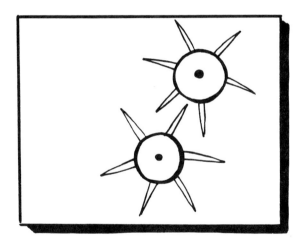

- Cardboard gears: Children make cardboard gears of various sizes. They can place them on thick cardboard or on a board with nails or pins. Let the children arrange them so that they move each other (Figure 94).

Figure 94

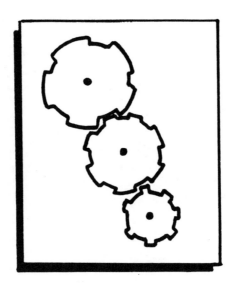

- Old clocks: Bring old clocks and other machines to school. Let the children take them apart and find the gears.
- How toys work: Place several toys that use gears, wheels, and pulleys on a tray. Music boxes that show the inside workings, a jack-in-the-box, wheel toys, water wheels, and pounding boxes are toys that can be used. Children sort them by the type of simple machine used in each.
- Matching foods and pictures: Have five to eight examples of white foods (apples, potatoes, onions, bread, radishes, bananas, etc.) in small dishes that are numbered. These foods should be cut into small cubes. Children taste the foods with toothpicks and match the picture of the food to the number.
- Sound match: Place single objects, such as a rock, a paper clip, and a pencil eraser, in individual plastic eggs. Place another set of the same objects in separate box lids. Children shake each egg and match it to the real object.
- Smell match: Children match jars containing flavoring extracts on cotton balls to pictures of the flavoring.

- Order by weight: Fill soft drink cans with varying amounts of sand and tape the tops closed. Children order them from lightest to heaviest.
- Telephone knocks: Purchase eight to ten feet of plastic tubing. Have children tell "knock-knock" jokes to each other from across the room.
- Make feely books: Have a page for each of the following: rough, smooth, bumpy, soft, and sticky. Children find pictures or objects or draw pictures to represent appropriate items in each category.
- Seed match: Use examples of seeds. Children match each type of seed to the word or picture of the plant.
- Planting seeds: Children plant seeds in different types of soil and measure their growth. They can then make a graph showing growth.
- Fruits and vegtables: Children sort pictures of fruits and vegetables into paper plates.
- Parts of plants: Children sort parts of real plants into flowers, stems, leaves, and roots.

MATHEMATICS CENTER

Rationale

The mathematics center is an area of the room where children play games that require mathematical thinking. Two of the best sources of games for this center are *Young Children Reinvent Arithmetic* (6) and *Young Children Continue to Reinvent Arithmetic, 2nd Grade* (7), both written by Kamii. These books describe how to sequence, play, and make appropriate mathematics games. Commercial games as well as teacher-made games are described.

Games for first grade stress the following objectives:

1. Adding addends up to 4 (1 + 1 to 4 + 4). The sums will equal up to 8.

2. Adding addends up to 6 (1 + 1 to 6 + 6). The sums will equal up to 12.
3. Adding doubles (2 + 2, 3 + 3, 5 + 5, etc.).
4. Set partitioning sums already known and of 10 (4 = 3 + 1, 2 + 2; 10 = 9 + 1, 8 + 2, 7 + 3, etc.).
5. "Thinking about 6, 7, 8, 9, as 5 + 1, 5 + 2, 5 + 3, and 5 + 4, and adding addends up to 10." Both 5 and 10 are used as pivot points in thinking. (6)

When children have played many games with addends up to 4, they begin to play games using regular dice with addends up to 6. After playing many games at this level, objectives 3, 4, and 5 may be developed without undue consideration for sequence.

Mathematics games should be truly games—not glorified worksheets. Games have a certain element of competition (even though competition is not stressed). They are fun, and children want to play them.

The games suggested by Kamii should be played without emphasis on written mathematics problems. After children spend a great deal of time playing games in first grade, the mental operations they need for addition will function without the need for written mathematics problems. Mathematics must be thought of as mental construction of a number system and not a body of skills to be learned.

Organization

The mathematics center should have shelves with individual spaces for 12 to 15 games. Two to three small tables where children can sit across from each other and play games provide the best arrangement for this center.

Activities

The following games are based on Kamii's first grade objectives (6). Many other games are described in her book.

Adding Addends Up to 4

- 40 pennies: Taking turns, two children throw dice with 1 to 4 dots, add the dots, and get pennies to fill the purse. Then the children take turns buying from a store, which is made of cards showing pictures of toys and other objects (stickers or workbook pictures).

- Trail game: Use any trail game board. Make two spinners with 1 to 4 dots. Taking turns, the children spin both spinners, add the dots, and move the number of spaces toward the end.

Adding Addends Up to 6

- Fill the cup: Each child has two dice and a large plastic cup. Taking turns, they roll, add the dice, and get chips for each number (for example, $3 + 4 = 7$ chips). They place chips in the plastic cup. The first person to fill the cup wins. (We let the children decide when the cups are full. The negotiating that takes place concerning who wins is most interesting.)

Adding Doubles

- Trail game doubles: Use any trail game with at least 80 spaces. Children roll one die, double the die, and move that number of spaces. The first child to reach the end of the trail wins the game.

- Doubles Bingo: This game requires game cards, a die, and buttons (or other small objects) to cover numbers on the cards. Make cards with 16 squares (4 $\times$ 4). Write one number—2, 4, 6, 8, 10 or 12 (the doubles of the numbers on the die)—on each of the 16 squares. The numbers should be placed randomly on each card (and the numbers on each card should be in a different order). Children take turns rolling the die. Each child doubles the number on the die and covers the sum on his or her card. The first child to cover a row, column, or diagonal is the winner.

Figure 95

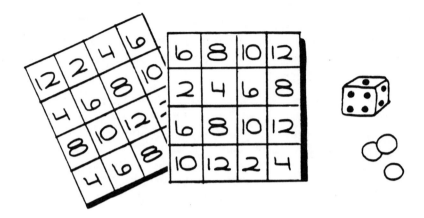

Set Partitioning Sums to 10

- Ten Concentration: Children lay out 28 playing cards, ace through 9, in four rows of seven cards. The first player turns over two cards. If the cards add up to 10, the player keeps the cards. The player with the most pairs wins.

Thinking about 6, 7, 8, 9, as 5 + 1, 5 + 2, 5 + 3, etc.

- Tic-Tac-Toe: Children play Tic-Tac-Toe, keeping score with tally marks.

ACTIVE PRIMARY CENTERS

The active centers are often omitted because of lack of space but they can provide valuable learnings if included in the primary classroom. The active primary centers—art, blocks, dramatic play, and music, are extensions of the preprimary centers discussed in Chapter 4. Only a brief discussion of these centers is included here. For more information, see Chapter 4.

Blocks Center

Unit blocks are often thought to be materials for kindergarten classrooms, but six-, seven-, and eight-year-old children benefit greatly from block building. Block building provides a means for children to represent understandings in social studies, science, reading, and mathematics. Block constructions are left out for longer periods of time so that play can be extended. As an outgrowth of social studies, children can build their school, homes, and streets as they explore mapping skills. Building farms, suburbs, cities, etc., children build their own community. Neighboring farms, cities, and communities can be constructed. In the art center, children can design facades for homes, stores, and schools. People, as well as trees and signs, made from pipe cleaners or tongue depressors can be used with the buildings. As children play with the buildings, they create the interrelationships and interdependencies of people, which are major social studies concepts.

Field trips to space centers, airports, zoos, post offices, banks, and factories can be built in blocks to help children rethink experiences. In science, blocks provide a place to explore pulleys, levers, wheels, inclined planes, and magnets.

As an outgrowth of reading, the blocks center provides an area where children can build story settings and reenact stories. Children can make props in the art center, build settings in blocks, and share the story with the classroom by moving the characters as they tell the story.

If unit blocks are not available or require more room than is available, smaller table-top blocks can be used in much the same way as the unit blocks.

Dramatic Play Center

The primary dramatic play center facilitates learnings in several curriculum areas. In economics, children can pretend to be clerks and customers in stores: mathematical understandings

163

are enhanced as children buy and sell. History comes to life as children dramatize Columbus's voyage or the first Thanksgiving.

As children mature in second and third grades, they are able to role play at higher levels. (Dramatic play becomes creative dramatics, using stories and situations as a basis for the dramatizations.) Conflict situations related to peer pressure, friendships, and family can be enacted. Stories from reading can be dramatized. One of the major differences between preprimary and primary dramatic play is the extent to which children use written language. Charts such as those in Figure 96 can be used more effectively at the primary level. Roles can be assumed and carried out more intensely. Because children think through action, dramatic play provides an excellent way of making content meaningful.

Music Center

Even though most primary classrooms have separate music teachers, children of this age benefit greatly from a music center. The activities for this center focus on developing an appreciation of various types of music, playing instruments, moving to music, studying musical notation, and listening to music related to social studies. Children are able to read or listen to tapes about the lives of famous composers as well as listen to their compositions.

Art Center

The art activities discussed in Chapter 4 continue to provide opportunites for primary-age children. As the children mature, their use of these art materials moves from exploration toward true self-expression.

The primary art center, much like the blocks center, is set up similar to the preprimary art center. Materials for drawing, collage, gluing, cutting, printing, constructing, and sculpting

Figure 96

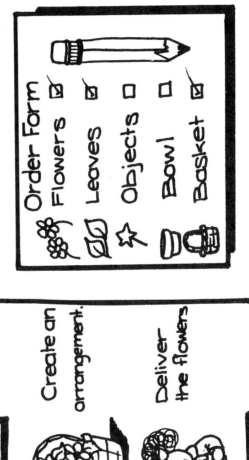

Order Form

Flowers ☑
Leaves ☑
Objects ☐
Bowl ☐
Basket ☑

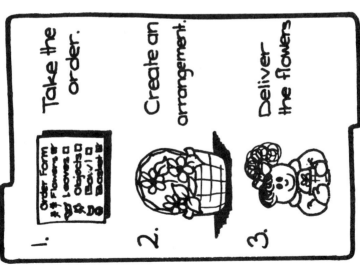

1. Take the order.

2. Create an arrangement.

3. Deliver the flowers

should be available at all times. We say "at all times" because by the time a child is six to eight years of age, and especially if he has had previous art center experiences, the art center becomes a place where he goes to represent, reconstruct, and create his own ideas. The ideas are usually an outgrowth of the child's personal experiences. Often subject matter studied in social studies, science, and reading provides the stimulus for art projects.

The major challenge found in this center is in organizing the many materials for ready access. Collage materials, such as sewing tape, pieces of fabric, ribbons, seeds, macaroni, pine cones, various styrofoam packing shapes, pebbles, shells, pipe cleaners, bottle caps, etc., are wonderful additions for children to use in their artwork, but can be a cluttered mess if not organized thoughtfully. See-through boxes used for sorting nails are wonderful for sorting small objects, such as seeds and shells. They can be hung on the wall for ready use. Hardware stores and discount stores often sell these storage containers. If many materials are provided and stored for easy access, children can unleash their imaginations to create wonderful works of art.

Shelves are essential for storage. Plastic bins and boxes can be used for larger art materials. Thought must be given to the storage of magazines, paper of all kinds (tissue, wallpaper, construction, scrap, foil, wax), felt-tip markers, crayons, tempera, paintbrushes, etc.

From time to time the teacher might suggest topics for the art center. All of the topics should revolve around the child and usually show action. Some interesting topics for the age are

> My Family Has Fun
> I Play with My Pet
> I Go to the Store
> We Play on the Playground
> I Am Going to Dress Up on Halloween
> I Lost My Tooth
> The First Thing I'll Do on Christmas Day
> I'm Going Riding

In addition to expressive art, the primary art curriculum should include famous artists. Young children can begin to understand line, shape, space, light, shade, texture, and color by looking at famous works of art. Some excellent sources for art appreciation for children are listed at the end of the chapter.

RESOURCE BOOKS

The following books are good resources for primary learning centers. Some of these books have activities that must be changed from teacher-directed to learning center activities.

Fine Arts

Burton, Leon, and William Hughes. *Music Play: Learning Activities for Young Children.* Menlo Park, Calif.: Addison-Wesley, 1979.

_____ . *Songs for Music Play.* Menlo Park, Calif.: Addison-Wesley, 1980.

Elkins, Pat. *Weekday Early Education Art Idea Book.* Nashville: Broadman Press, 1978.

Hodgson, Harriet. *Artworks.* Palo Alto, Calif: Monday Morning Books, 1986.

Striker, Susan, and Edward Kimmel. *The Second Anti-Coloring Book.* New York: Holt, Rinehart & Winston, 1984.

Wolf, Aline D. *Mommy, It's a Renoir!* Altoona, Pa.: Parent Child Press, 1986.

Language Arts

Barbe, Walter B., and Brenda P. Shields. *Reading Skills Check List and Activities: First Level.* West Nyack, N.Y.: Center for Applied Research in Education, 1976.

Carson, Patti, and Janet Dellosa. *All Aboard for Readiness Skills.* Akron, Ohio: Carson-Dellosa Publishing, 1977.

Cromwell, Liz, Dixie Hibner, and John R. Faitel, comps. *Finger Frolics.* Rev. ed. Livonia, Mich.: Partner Press, 1983.

Dowell, Ruth I. *Move Over Mother Goose!* Mount Rainier, Md.: Gryphon House, 1987.

Evans, Joy, and Jo Ellen Moore. *How to Make Books with Children.* Monterey, Calif.: Evans-Moore, 1985.

Finch, Karen. *File Folder Games.* Greensboro, N.C.: Carson-Dellosa Publishing, 1990.

Graham, Terry L. *Fingerplays and Rhymes for Always and Sometimes.* Atlanta: Humanics Ltd., 1986.

Grayson, Marion. *Let's Do Finger-Plays* . Washington, D.C.: Robert B. Luce, 1962.

Greff, Kasper N., and Eunice N. Askov. *Learning Centers: An Ideabook for Reading and Language Arts.* Dubuque, Iowa: Kendall/Hunt, 1974.

Krause, Claudia. *Alphabetivities: 175 Ready-to-Use Activities from A to Z.* West Nyack, N.Y.: Center for Applied Research in Education, 1986.

Petreshene, Susan S. *Complete Guide to Learning Centers.* Palo Alto, Calif.: Pendragon House, 1978.

_____ . *Complete Guide to Learning Centers Supplement.* Palo Alto, Calif.: Pendragon House, 1978.

Saludis, Anthony J. *Language Arts Activities.* 2d ed. Dubuque, Iowa: Kendall/Hunt, 1977.

Silverstein, Shel. *Where the Sidewalk Ends.* New York: Harper & Row, 1974.

Spache, Evelyn B. *Reading Activities for Child Involvement.* Boston: Allyn & Bacon, 1973.

Sull, Elizabeth C. *Children's Book Activities Kit.* West Nyack, N.Y.: Center for Applied Research in Education, 1988.

Wilmes, Liz, and Dick Wilmes. *Imagination Stretchers.* Elgin, Ill.: Building Blocks, 1985.

Mathematics

Kamii, Constance. *Young Children Reinvent Arithmetic: Implications of Piaget's Theory.* New York: Teachers College Press, 1985.

_____ . *Young Children Continue to Reinvent Arithmetic, 2d Grade: Implications of Piaget's Theory.* New York: Teachers College Press, 1989.

Science

Forte, Imogene, and Joy MacKenzie. *Creative Science Experiences for the Young Child.* Rev.ed. Nashville: Incentive Publications, 1983.

Lowery, Lawrence, and Carol Verbeeth. *Explorations in Physical Science.* Belmont, Calif.: David S. Lake, 1987.

Markle, Sandra. *Primary Science Sampler.* Santa Barbara, Calif.: Learning Works, 1980.

Moore, Jo Ellen, and Joy Evans. *Learning About Plants.* Monterey, Calif.: Evans-Moore, 1987.

_____ . *Simple Science Experiments.* Monterey, Calif.: Evan-Moor, 1987.

Poppe, Carol A., and Nancy A. Van Matre. *Science Learning Centers for the Primary Grades.* West Nyack, N.Y.: Center for Applied Research in Education, 1985.

_____ . *K–3 Science Activities Kit.* West Nyack, N.Y.: Center for Applied Research in Education, 1988.

VanCleave, Janice Pratt. *Teaching the Fun of Physics.* New York: Prentice-Hall Press, 1987.

Social Studies

Cabbalene, Jane, and Derele Whondley. *Children Around the World.* Atlanta: Humanics Ltd., 1983.

Crary, Elizabeth. *Kids Can Cooperate.* Seattle: Parenting Press, 1979.

Poppe, Carol A., and Nancy A. VanMatre. *Social Studies Learning Centers for the Primary Grades.* West Nyack, N.Y.: Center for Applied Research in Education, 1990.

General

Ard, Linda, and Mabel Pitts, eds. *Room to Grow: How to Create Quality Early Childhood Environments.* Austin: Texas Association for the Education of Young Children, in press.

Forte, Imogene, and Joy Mackenzie. *Nooks, Crannies and Corners* Rev. ed. Nashville: Incentive Publications, 1978.

Gottshall, Dottie, comp. *Primary Learning Center Activities.* Nacogdoches, Tex.: Stephen F. Austin State University Printing, n.d.

Herr, Judy, and Yvonne Libby. *Designing Creative Materials for Young Children.* Orlando, Fla: Harcourt Brace Jovanovich, 1990.

Petreshene, Susan S. *Mind Joggers.* West Nyack, N.Y.: Center for Applied Research in Education, 1985.

Chapter 6

WHERE TO START

For the traditional teacher, the task of changing to a learning center classroom may seem overwhelming. It is important to remember that one does not move from a traditional classroom teaching style to learning centers overnight. This may lead to chaos and confusion for both the children and the teacher. The transition to a child-directed classroom is a slow, gradual process (3).

The teacher should consider starting with one or two centers, choosing centers that require materials that are readily available and involve a minimum of mess. For example, in the preprimary classroom, the library center and the table games center may be used to begin. Most teachers have access to library books, and by adding a few storytelling props and comfortable pillows, the library center is ready for use. New activities and materials can be added during the year as they are developed. Also, most preprimary classrooms have manipulative puzzles and games that can be used to start a table games center. In the primary classroom, the library center can again be set up easily, and the creative writing and mathmatics centers would need only a few basic materials, such as notebooks for journal writing, to get started.

It is better to do a few centers well than to overextend yourself and try to do too many centers too soon with too few materials. It takes time and resources to build files of materials. Many traditional materials can be restructured for learning center use. Many teachers take several years to develop learning center classrooms. By setting realistic goals, such as developing two centers a year, teachers can implement this approach easily.

When using only two centers, the teacher might need to temporarily develop a different organizational system since there will not be enough center spaces for all children. During this transitional phase, the primary teacher might work with one small reading group and have the other children work in the library and the creative writing centers and do seatwork activities. As more centers are added, children will have more choices. As the teacher and the children become used to the learning center format, more centers can be added throughout the year or in succeeding years. This allows the teacher time to develop additional materials for use in the classroom.

Once a total learning center classroom has been established, each year the process of introducing the centers to a new group of children begins again. It is still best to start with just a few centers. Preview the rules and activities carefully and give children time to learn how to choose centers, work on their own, and clean up. New centers can be previewed and added each week as children show that they are ready.

In year-round programs, such as ours, it is not necessary to reintroduce the centers each year. As new children come into the program throughout the year, other children provide models and assistance to ease the transition. Because the centers are self-selected and provide active learning, children maintain a high interest level even during summer months.

It is important to remember that learning centers provide the major learning time of the day. They are not rewards or free play. Centers should not be viewed as a reward for good behavior after other teacher-directed activities are completed. When learning centers are viewed as reinforcement, the very children who need centers the most may be denied the opportunity as punishment or because they are slower in completing their work.

The use of learning centers in the early childhood classroom is a continuing process. Any changes that the teacher makes to move toward more child-directed, rather than teacher-directed, activity is a positive step toward more developmentally appropriate practice. However, even the most experienced learning center teacher will change learning centers from year to year to meet the needs and interest of her children. Each teacher must choose a method of organizing and implementing learning centers that she finds comfortable and appropriate. We have shared with you one way that we have found to be successful, but our program is continuously evolving. Learning centers are not static, but dynamic. They develop and change over time, as do the teacher and the children.

BIBLIOGRAPHY

1. Bredekamp, Sue, ed. *Developmentally Appropriate Practice in Early Childhood Programs Serving Children from Birth Through Age 8.* Exp. ed. Washington, D.C.: National Association for the Education of Young Children, 1987.

2. Dewey, John, and Evelyn Dewey. *Schools of Tomorrow.* New York: E.P. Dutton & Co., 1915.

3. Forte, Imogene, and Joy Mackenzie. *Nooks, Crannies and Corners: Learning Centers for Creative Classrooms.* Rev. ed. Nashville: Incentive Publications, 1978.

4. Hirsch, Elisabeth S., ed. *The Block Book.* Washington, D.C.: National Association for the Education of Young Children, 1974.

5. Howard, A. Eugene. *The Integrated Approach Design.* Nacogdoches, Tex.: Early Childhood Consultant Services, 1975.

6. Kamii, Constance. *Young Children Reinvent Arithmetic: Implications of Piaget's Theory.* New York: Teachers College Press, 1985.

7. _____. *Young Children Continue to Reinvent Arithmetic, 2nd Grade: Implications of Piaget's Theory.* New York: Teachers College Press, 1989.

8. Kohl, MaryAnn F. *Mudworks: Creative Clay, Dough, and Modeling Experiences.* Bellingham, Wash.: Bright Ring Publishing, 1989.

9. *Now You're Talking: Techniques That Extend Conversations.* Portland, Ore.: Educational Productions, 1987.

10. *Oh Say What They See: An Introduction to Indirect Language Stimulation Techniques.* Portland, Ore.: Educational Productions, 1984.

11. Pattillo, Janice. "First and Second Grade Classrooms." In *Room to Grow: How to Create Quality Early Childhood Environments,* edited by Linda Ard and Mabel Pitts. Austin, Tex.: Texas Association for the Education of Young Children, in press.

12. Petreshene, Susan S. *Complete Guide to Learning Centers.* Palo Alto, Calif.: Pendragon House, 1978.

175

13. ____. *Complete Guide to Learning Centers: Supplement.* Palo Alto, Calif.: Pendragon House, 1978.

14. Piaget, Jean. *To Understand Is to Invent.* 1948. Reprint. New York: Grossman Publishers, 1973.

15. Samuels, Shirley C. *Enhancing Self-Concept in Early Childhood.* New York: Human Sciences Press, 1977.

16. Smilansky, Sara. "Can Adults Facilitate Play in Children? Theoretical and Practical Considerations." In *Play: The Child Strives Toward Self-Realization,* edited by Georgianna Engstrom. Washington, D.C.: National Association for the Education of Young Children, 1971.

17. Veatch, Jeannette, Florence Sawicki, Geraldine Elliott, Eleanor Flake, and Janis Blakey. *Key Words to Reading: The Language Experience Approach Begins.* 2d ed. Columbus, Ohio: Charles E. Merrill, 1979.

18. Wolfgang, Charles H., Bea Mackender, and Mary E. Wolfgang. *Growing and Learning Through Play.* New York: McGraw-Hill, 1981.